MW01687105

HELL, HIGHWATER & HARD CASES

Books by the same author

The Territory Rouseabout and Other Humourous Verses
The Packhorse Drover
In Leichhardt's Footsteps

HELL, HIGHWATER & HARD CASES

BRUCE SIMPSON

ABC BOOKS

This book is dedicated to the memory of all those tough characters and hard cases who helped tame the outback.

Published by ABC Books for the
AUSTRALIAN BROADCASTING CORPORATION
GPO Box 9994 Sydney NSW 2001

Copyright © Bruce Simpson 1999

First published October 1999

All rights reserved. No part of this publication may be reproduced, stored in a retrieval system or transmitted in any form or by any means, electronic, mechanical, photocopying, recording or otherwise, without the prior written permission of the Australian Broadcasting Corporation.

National Library of Australia
Cataloguing-in-Publication entry
Simpson, Bruce (Bruce F.).

Hell, highwater and hard cases.

ISBN 0 7333 0795 7.

1. Frontier and pioneer life—Australia—Anecdotes. 2. Frontier and pioneer life—Australia—History. 3. Country life—Australia—Anecdotes. 4. Country life—Australia—History. I. Australian Broadcasting Corporation. II. Title.

994

Designed by Jim Shepherd
Edited by Margaret Bowman
Set in 10/14 pt Cheltenham by
Midland Typesetters, Maryborough, Victoria
Colour separations by Finsbury, Adelaide
Printed and bound in Australia by
Southwood Press, Marrickville

5 4 3 2 1

Contents

Acknowledgments

There are many people who have helped me put together this book. My sincere thanks to the following: Jack Cunningham of Brisbane, Qld; Mrs Lola Rowe of Mildura, Vic; Cecil Teece of Normanton, Qld; Peter Treloar of Delaney Creek, Qld; Peter Knowls of Winton, Qld; Rod Bellette of Patterson Lakes, Vic; Kerry Kendall of Middlemount, Qld; Jim 'Ringer' Edwards of Gin Gin, WA; Jim Pearson of Gatton, Qld; Merv Rogers of Charters Towers, Qld; Luke McCall of Batlow, NSW; Roy Hulbert of Bangalow, NSW; Bob Isles of Redcliffe, Qld; Lucky Forrester of Strathpine, Qld; Barry Desailly of North Ward, Qld; Les Huddy of Mt Isa, Qld; Gordon Gaffney of Tamworth, NSW; Ray Webster of Landsborough, Qld; George Booth Jnr of Port Douglas, Qld; Alf Chambers of Taroom, Qld; Darell Lewis of Canberra, ACT; Mick Bailey of Broken Hill, NSW; Tidly Treffett of Charters Towers, Qld; the late Frank Uhr of Finch Hatton, Qld; Alex Logan of Kumbia, Qld; Ernie McCarthy of Pine Creek, NT; Eddie Hackman of Rockhampton, Qld; Herb Huemiller of Barcaldine, Qld; Ian Tait of Koumala, Qld; the late Jack Gardner of Caloundra, Qld; Bob Kirk of Herbert Downs, Qld; Mal Debney of Glenormiston Station, Qld; the late Walter Lloyd of Boulia, Qld; Bob Howard of Caboolture, Qld; Ross Ratcliffe of The Willows, Qld; Jeff Simpson of Stanthorpe, Qld; Merv Thomas of Landsborough, Qld; Mick Thomas of Barcaldine, Qld; Noel Thompson of D'Aguilar, Qld; Eugene Costin, of Brunette Downs, NT; Barney Bellford of Eukey, Qld; the late Bobby McDonald of Barcaldine, Qld; Tony Roberts of Canberra, ACT; the late Gilbert Macintosh of Mt Isa; Qld; Tom Cusack of Mittiebah Station, NT; Noel 'Pic' Willetts of Camooweal, Qld; Rodney Mosted of Camooweal, Qld; John Chaplain of Cloncurry, Qld; Jack Drake of Eukey, Qld; Ab Teece of Cloncurry, Qld; Mrs Ada Devereaux of Brisbane, Qld; Ron Easey of Petrie, Qld; Chris Gladwell and Jim Cuming of the Stockmen's Hall of Fame office, Brisbane, Qld; Colin Campbell of Mitchell, Qld; Sam Fuller Jnr of Mitchell, Qld; Bill Alexander of Marian Downs, Qld; Blue Ellis of Bankstown, NSW; Ray Gillham of Suttor Creek Station, Qld; Lyn Craig of Eton, Qld; Laurie Hansen of Finch Hatton, Qld; the staff of the John Oxley and State Library, Brisbane, Qld; Steve Millard of the NAPCO office, Brisbane, Qld; Jim Kennedy of Brisbane, Qld; Graham Murchie of Stanthorpe, Qld; Lloyd Linson-Smith of Oakey, Qld;

Ian Tinney of Brisbane, Qld; Keith Haughton of Narangba, Qld; Bob Nash of Pinnacle, Qld; Peter Isles of Redcliffe, Qld; the late Fred Holm of Winton, Qld; Larry Holm of Townsville, Qld; Brian Holm of Winton, Qld; Bill Moore of Redcliffe, Qld; Mick Cheadle, now of Millungera Station, Qld; Graham McKerrow of Weona Station, Winton, Qld; Matt Masterson of Mareeba, Qld; Alex Long of Caboolture, Qld; Bobbie Buchanan of Berry Springs, NT; Ron Bates of Gatton, Qld; and lastly my son Ranald for his technical help in producing the manuscript for this book.

All poems in the book with the exception of 'Where the Pelican Builds' are by the author.

About the Author

Bruce Simpson has lived the Outback legend. Born in Australia's bush heart, he drove cattle for thousands of miles in the tracks of ghostly legends before him, collecting stories and writing poems as he went. And he is still living the legend—leading two rugged expeditions in search of Leichhardt and winning frequent awards as a bush laureate. He honed his craft beside the campfire, celebrating a life which has dwindled like the campfires behind him, ensuring that our past is not forgotten.

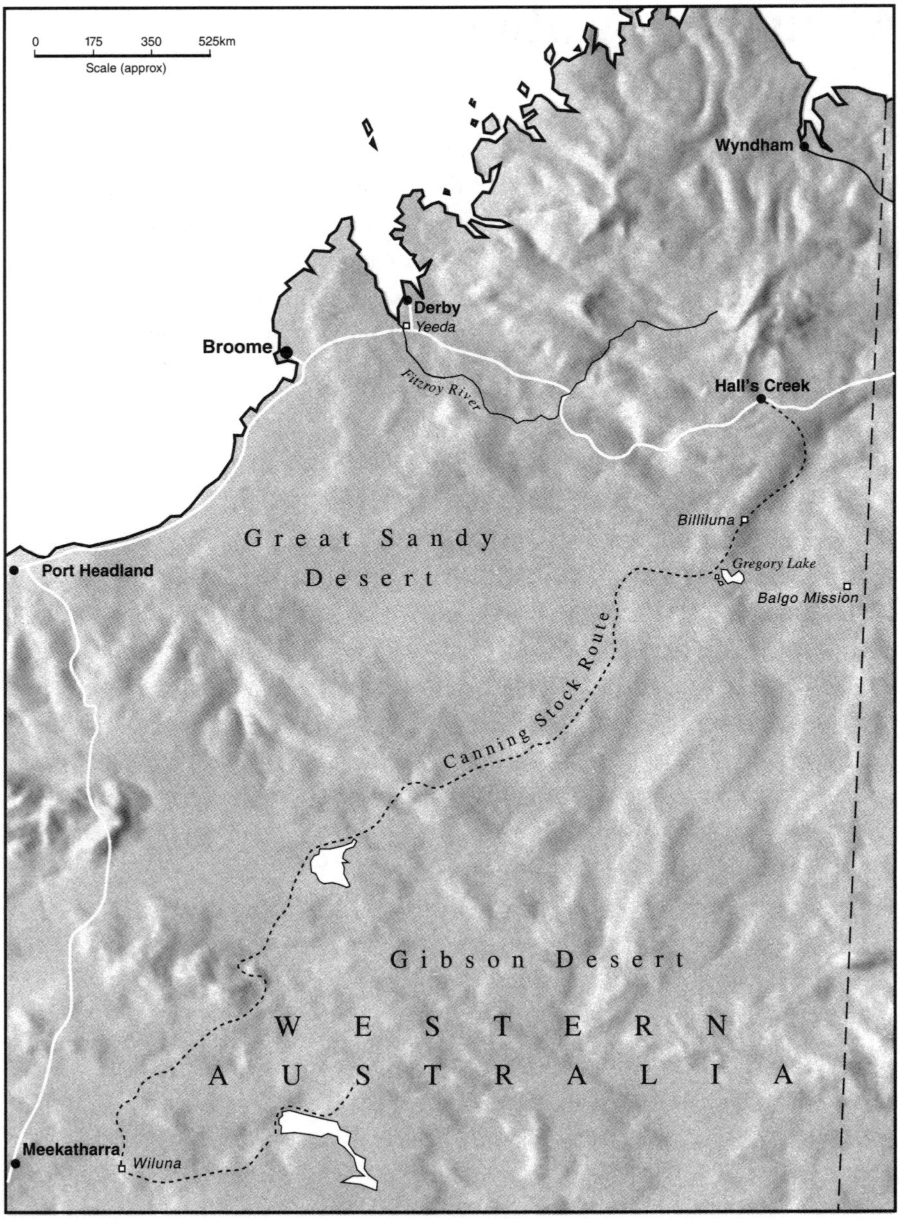

0
175
350
525km
Scale (approx)
Wyndham
Derby
Yeeda
Broome
Fitzroy River
Hall's Creek
Billiluna
Gregory Lake
Balgo Mission
Great Sandy Desert
Port Headland
Canning Stock Route
Gibson Desert
WESTERN AUSTRALIA
Meekatharra
Wiluna

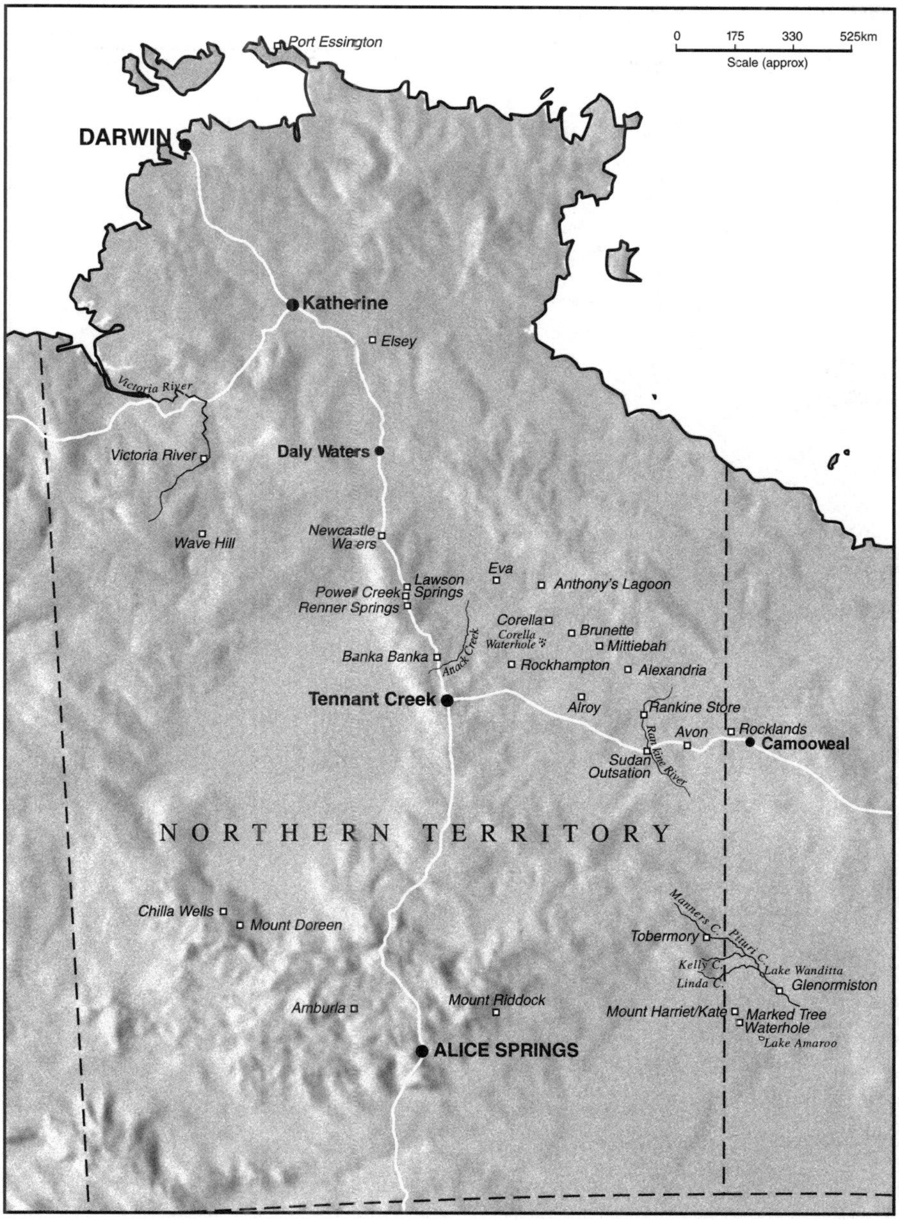

0
175
330
525km
Scale (approx)
Port Essington
DARWIN
Katherine
Elsey
Victoria River
Victoria River
Daly Waters
Newcastle Waters
Wave Hill
Eva
Lawson Springs
Powell Creek
Anthony's Lagoon
Renner Springs
Corella
Corella Waterhole
Brunette
Mittiebah
Banka Banka
Anack Creek
Rockhampton
Alexandria
Tennant Creek
Alroy
Rankine Store
Avon
Rocklands
Camooweal
Sudan Outsation
Rankine River
NORTHERN TERRITORY
Chilla Wells
Mount Doreen
Manners C.
Tobermory
Pituri C.
Kelly C.
Lake Wanditta
Linda C.
Glenormiston
Amburla
Mount Riddock
Mount Harriet/Kate
Marked Tree Waterhole
Lake Amaroo
ALICE SPRINGS

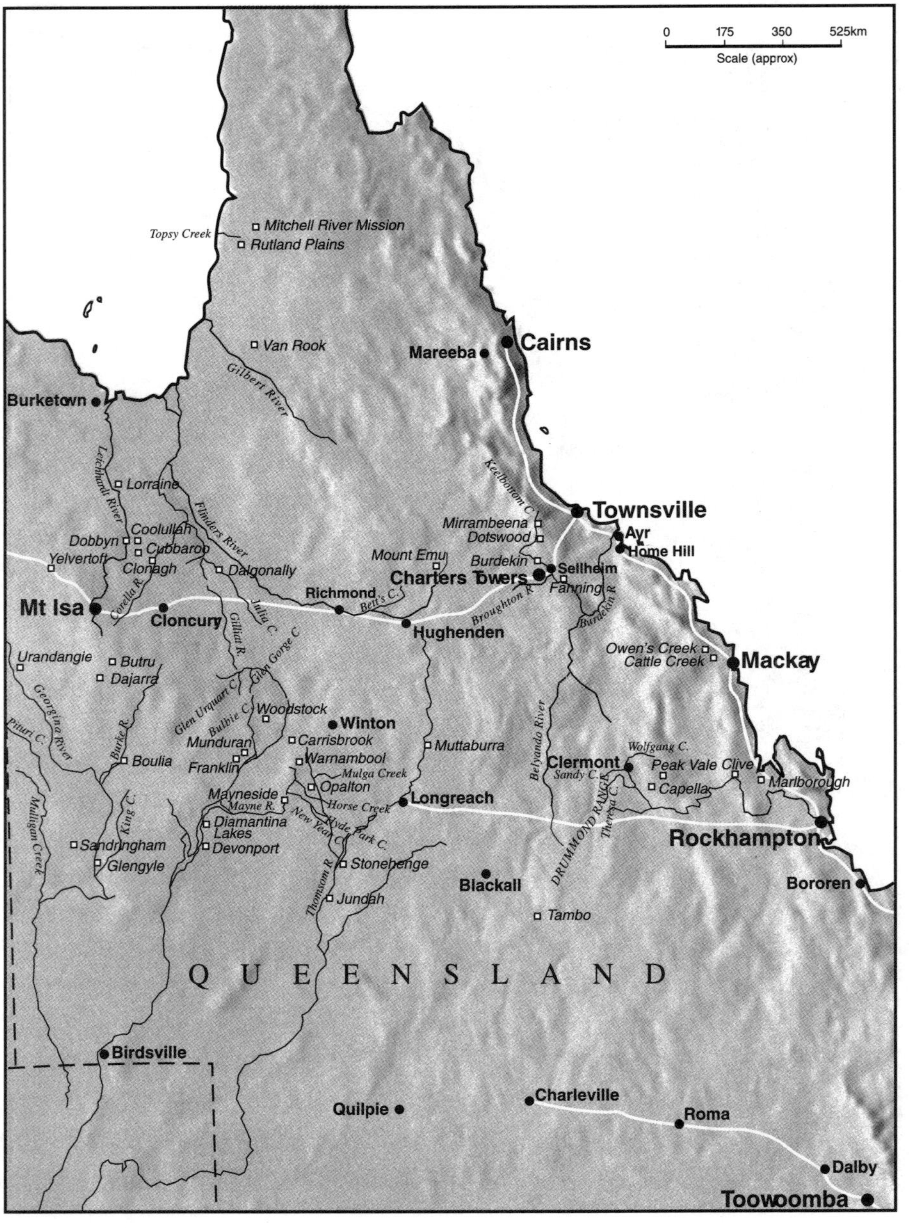

0 175 350 525km
Scale (approx)
Topsy Creek
Mitchell River Mission
Rutland Plains
Van Rook
Mareeba
Cairns
Burketown
Gilbert River
Leichhardt River
Lorraine
Flinders River
Keelbottom C.
Townsville
Mirrambeena
Dotswood
Ayr
Home Hill
Dobbyn
Coolullah
Cubbaroo
Clonagh
Yelvertoft
Dalgonally
Mount Emu
Burdekin
Sellheim
Charters Towers
Fanning
Corella R.
Mt Isa
Cloncurry
Richmond
Bett's C.
Julia C.
Broughton R.
Burdekin R.
Hughenden
Gilliat R.
Glen Gorge C.
Urandangie
Butru
Dajarra
Owen's Creek
Cattle Creek
Mackay
Georgina River
Glen Urquart C.
Bulbie C.
Woodstock
Winton
Pituri C.
Burke R.
Munduran
Carrisbrook
Muttaburra
Belyando River
Boulia
Franklin
Warnambool
Mulga Creek
Opalton
Wolfgang C.
Clermont
Sandy C.
Peak Vale
Clive
Capella
Marlborough
Mayneside
Mayne R.
Horse Creek
Longreach
Mulligan Creek
King C.
Diamantina Lakes
New Year C.
Hyde Park C.
Sandringham
Devonport
Theresa C.
DRUMMOND RANGE
Rockhampton
Glengyle
Thomson R.
Stonehenge
Blackall
Bororen
Jundah
Tambo
QUEENSLAND
Birdsville
Charleville
Quilpie
Roma
Dalby
Toowoomba

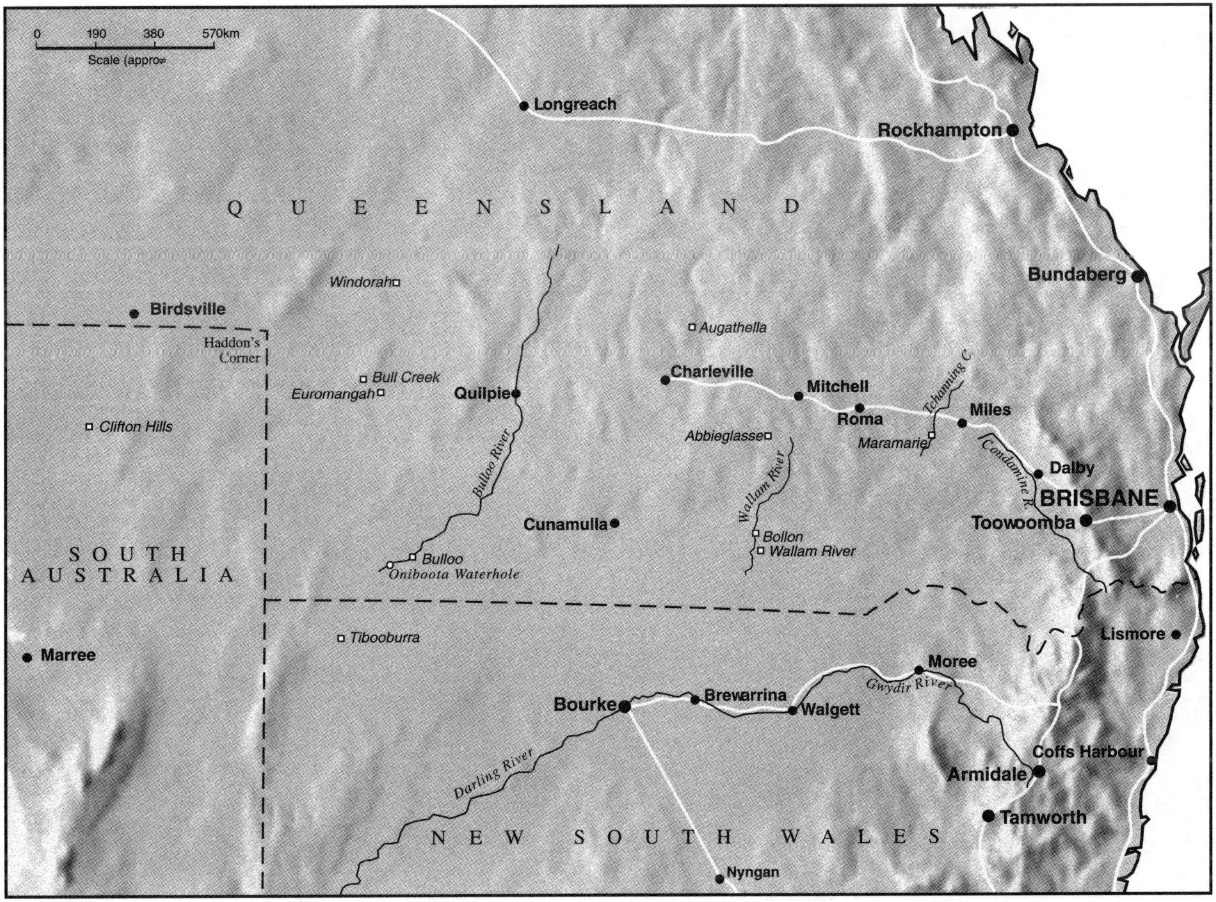
0 190 380 570km
Scale (appro≠
Longreach
Rockhampton
Q U E E N S L A N D
Bundaberg
Windorah
Birdsville
Augathella
Haddon's Corner
Bull Creek
Euromangah
Quilpie
Charleville
Mitchell
Roma
Tchanning C
Miles
Clifton Hills
Abbieglasse
Maramarie
Condamine R.
Dalby
Bulloo River
Wallam River
BRISBANE
Toowoomba
Cunamulla
Bollon
Wallam River
S O U T H
A U S T R A L I A
Bulloo
Oniboota Waterhole
Tibooburra
Lismore
Marree
Moree
Gwydir River
Bourke
Brewarrina
Walgett
Coffs Harbour
Armidale
Darling River
Tamworth
N E W S O U T H W A L E S
Nyngan

The author on Berlin, a rough horse on Alexandria stockcamp.

Death on the Barkly

One of the worst droughts experienced in the Territory was in 1952. Early in the year I left Camooweal with a packhorse plant en route to Eva Downs. Despite knowing that the Tableland had claimed the lives of many, the trip held no terrors for me; I was confident that I knew the area fairly well, as I had worked for just on two years in the stockcamp on Alexandria and had crossed the Tableland on the stockroute. I had a good mate with me, Bruce Hanson, whom I had worked with on Glenormiston. He was a good ringer but had been away from the game for a few years—and he was no tracker—so it was always my job to do the horse-tailing and find horses that were away from the main mob.

With the season being so dry and horse feed so scarce, this was necessary almost every morning. We worked as a team; my mate would be throwing the packs on while I went after the strays. This was not a problem until I developed sandy blight about the time we got to Lawn Creek on Alexandria. Sandy blight can be a real curse in the bush. Every morning it took me a few minutes with a handkerchief and a quart pot of warm salty water to get my eyelids separated. My eye became progressively weaker and reacted strongly to bright sunlight, making tracking lost horses something of a torment, and I found I constantly had to dismount to check tracks.

I hoped to get something to relieve the curse from Dick Carter at the Rankine store, but he could offer me nothing to relieve the condition of my eyes. When needs must the devil drives, so we kept going. I tied a handkerchief over my eyes and rode blind behind the horses as we moved from camp to camp. Bruce had a go at finding missing horses, and he did his best, but if horses cleared out, Bruce did not know the country, so I decided to carry on.

We camped one night out from a stockroute bore. Next morning there were four horses away. After a quick breakfast of corned meat and damper, I helped Bruce start to pack up. Then I noticed he had a horse we called Match Box tied up. He was usually hard to catch and, being in a hurry most mornings, we had not ridden him a lot. I decided he was overdue for a bit of work and told my mate I would take him to look for the missing horses. I saddled Match Box then filled a waterbag and hung it around his neck.

I told Bruce to go on to the next water when he had finished packing the rest of the horses. As I was confident the strays would not be too far away, I said I would catch him up. I then gave my eyes a quick bathe and rode off. Half blind as I was, it took me the best part of half an hour to pick up where the missing horses had left the main mob. Normally horses that split off will feed around and finish up not too far from the main mob. These four horses, however, seemed to have a definite destination in mind. Their tracks led off almost due west in a fairly straight line. This did make tracking them fairly easy, although I still had to dismount every few hundred metres to check their tracks. I used these moments to bathe my eyes from the waterbag.

After following the tracks for some seven kilometres, I dismounted and, satisfied the missing horses were still ahead of me, I wet my handkerchief from the waterbag and squatted down to clear my eyes, a rein lying loosely across one arm. Being hardly able to see, I did not notice the small goanna lying doggo beside me. When I moved, it took off and ran straight up my horse's front leg. There is nothing calculated to give a horse a bigger fright, and Match Box was no different. He pulled away, wheeled around and galloped off, leaving me sitting on the ground clutching a wet handkerchief.

I cursed, stood up and looked for the horse. I could see nothing. The sunlight danced like coloured lights through my misted vision. I scrabbled at my eyes with the hankie and looked again. I still could not see my mount.

I forced myself to remain calm and, crouching down, tried to pick him out against the wavering horizon. With a cry of relief, I saw the dim shape of the horse moving some 200 metres away to my right. He seemed to be heading back the way we had come. I stood up and realised I was still in a dangerous situation. I had to catch Match Box or I was in real trouble. My mate would be off to the next camp and would not miss me until late afternoon. He probably would not take any action until after dark or my riderless horse caught up with the plant. Realising the futility of trying to find me himself, he would be likely to ride to the nearest station for help. Tomorrow would be the earliest a search party could be organised and that could well be too late for me.

It was now almost midday, the sun was nearly overhead, and I was in no condition to walk a hundred metres in a straight line. I had to catch the horse, that was my only chance. I crouched down again and, yes, there he was, still walking back towards the camp we had left. I rose and started walking on a parallel course. I dared not go directly towards him lest he take fright and start trotting. I stumbled on, slowly gaining on my loose mount, resting now and again to clear my eyes with the rapidly drying handkerchief. It took me over half an hour to draw level with the horse. He had thankfully found a little dry grass, so that stopped his progress for a while.

Sandy blight is a debilitating condition, underfoot was loose, dry ground and I was beginning to feel the pinch. I decided it was now or never and I angled in towards the horse, which was still some distance away. Match Box looked at me and walked on. You bastard, I thought, this is a game of life or death and you're playing with me. I began talking to him and gradually edged a little closer. I knew it would be fatal to move quickly, and I was not sure how long I could keep up the pursuit. One eye was almost closed with the strain of looking into the glare. I cursed myself for a fool in riding a horse that I had known was hard to catch.

After a period that seemed like an eternity, I found myself in front of the horse. He was still about 30 metres away, and was looking at me. I sat down and caught my breath. I knew with this particular horse, one false move would undo all my good work.

Finally I stood up slowly and, trying not to stumble, walked slowly forward. Thankfully Match Box stood there until I quietly caught him. I patted him and lent against his shoulder. I was feeling done in and I knew for sure I would have been in trouble getting back on foot.

I bathed my eyes, had a drink of water and again cut the tracks of the missing plant horses. About an hour later I found them in a hollow in the downs. It was almost dark when I got to camp. I kept my misadventure to myself but it was a salutary lesson I never forgot.

Throughout the history of the Northern Territory, living conditions and lifestyle have taken a huge toll of human life. There have been shootings, spearings and other violent deaths inflicted by Territorians on their fellow beings. The Territory was an isolated and inhospitable frontier and, like all rough frontier regions, it attracted hard and often violent types of men.

It was accidental death, however, that claimed the greatest number of victims in the development of the Northern Territory. Of all the ways for a person to die, perishing from thirst is the cruelest. One area of the Territory, the Barkly Tableland, had a grisly reputation for visiting this form of agonising death on the unwary. People died of thirst in many parts of Australia, but it was the Tableland that was the undisputed killer.

On 29 August 1883 a bullocky named Joseph Martins was killed by Aborigines. It was the beginning of a chain of events that would result in the death by thirst of six members of a police party, a catastrophe that sent shock waves through the administration of the Territory. The murder took place at Lawson's Springs, north of Powell's Creek. Martins and his mate John Rees, together with an Aboriginal boy named Gumen, had unyoked the bullocks and had taken them into the spring to water them. After watering the bullocks, they decided to stay at Lawson's Springs that night. A small group of bush Aborigines, who appeared to be friendly, were also camped there.

At about 10.30 p.m. Rees was awakened by a disturbance. He heard Gumen shout out in alarm and, jumping from his swag, saw an Aborigine standing over Martins with a heavy firestick. He fired his revolver at the man, who disappeared. Going over to Martins, Rees found that he had been bludgeoned to death. No motive was reported for the murder. A native woman may have been involved, although the Wagata tribe, whose country encompassed the Attack Creek area, had been known to kill before.

A punitive patrol was organised, led by Mounted Constable Shirley. With him were a number of trackers, as well as John Rees and A.W. Giles, from the Overland Telegraph station at Powell's Creek. Giles, who had a reasonable knowledge of the local Aboriginal language, acted as interpreter. The trackers attached to the patrol picked up the tracks of the suspect group on 22 September. These tracks were followed to north of Newcastle Waters.

While the patrol was temporarily halted on 1 October, the Aborigines attacked. Boomerangs and spears were thrown and were answered with rifle fire. No casualties were inflicted on members of the party and the Aborigines slipped away into the thick Bullwaddy scrub. Rees and Gumen recognised some of the attackers as men wanted for the killing of Martins. The tracks of the wanted group then led south towards Attack Creek.

It was at this point that a rumour concerning the murder of a party of whites began to gain credence. On 5 September Harry Redford, J.F. Uhr, P. Kelly and a man named Macansh had left Attack Creek to travel to Corella Station. The men, all experienced bushmen, had started out at 2 p.m. and faced a dry stage of some 90 miles (144 kilometres). Nothing had been heard of the party since, although this should not have been surprising considering the lack of communications in that part of the world. The commissioner of police was concerned, however, and advised Mounted Constable Shirley to abandon the pursuit of the Aborigines who had killed Martins and investigate the possible murder of Redford's party. On 29 October an enlarged police patrol gathered at Attack Creek. With Constable Shirley were John Rees, A.W. Giles, John Hussey and brothers Arthur and George Phillips. Two police boys were included as trackers, making a total of eight. From this point on the story of the disastrous episode is based entirely on the report of A.W. Giles, the only white survivor.

Shirley intended to follow the tracks of Redford's party, and to shorten the dry stage he went out on the 30th with Rees, Giles and a tracker to try and find water east of Attack Creek. They took two packhorses with them; one of these, an aged horse in poor condition, carried water canteens. The small party travelled about 25 miles (40 kilometres) but found no water, so made a dry camp. Next day, Wednesday 31st, Rees found a native well 6 miles (10 kilometres) past the night camp. There were also some crabholes, or gilgais, around the well. This well became known as Rees's well, and played a major part in the tragedy. The party camped there that night, minus the water canteen horse, which had died during the day.

On Thursday 1 November, Shirley went back to Attack Creek and brought up the rest of the police party. The full patrol then camped at the well. Shirley apparently decided to spend 2 November in a reconnaissance of the area. More crabholes were found 2 miles (about 3 kilometres) to the east of the camp, and Redford's tracks were cut. On the 3rd he moved the patrol out to these crabholes and camped there. The patrol was now over 30 miles (48 kilometres) from Attack Creek. There had been plenty of horse feed around the camps and the patrol should have been in good shape to cover the dry stage ahead.

On Sunday 4 November Shirley led the patrol out from the crabholes and followed Redford's tracks for some 35 miles (56 kilometres). At 7 p.m. the party settled down in a dry camp. The next day, the 5th, things started to go wrong. The patrol left camp at 6.15 a.m. and proceeded along Redford's tracks. Later these tracks were lost and at 3 p.m. the patrol began searching a line of coolabahs in the hope of finding water. Shirley made camp at 5 p.m., having travelled only 25 miles (40 kilometres). In camp he advised the members of the party that he intended to return to Rees's well. There was only 3 gallons (13.5 litres) of water left.

In a very good season a large lake system forms in the Barkly region, covering parts of Anthony's Lagoon, Brunette Downs, Eva Downs and Rockhampton Downs. When these lakes dry back, it is very difficult to get to them; in a bad drought, it is impossible. In 1952 I took a job with the Chambers Brothers on Eva Downs. Most of the lake country was then dry but was covered in blue bush; this is excellent cattle feed. In an attempt to save the Eva herd, the Chambers boys decided to put down bores in the dry lake country. I helped Bill with the boring, using an old percussion plant. I then did the horsetailing, as Alf built the earth tanks with a horse team. It was astute management; the Eva Downs herd was saved. In a good season those bores were metres under water.

Had Shirley known the area, he would not have wasted time looking for water. Before turning back, all swags, heavy gear and the bulk of the rations were placed in trees to lighten the load on the packhorses. At 6.30 p.m., taking only the water and some light rations, the patrol set off to travel all night on the return journey to Rees's well. The party ran into thick scrub and Giles was convinced that Shirley was heading too far to the south. In the early morning he confronted the constable with his belief. After some argument, in which the other members backed Giles, Shirley turned more to the north. The party travelled another 10 miles (16 kilometres) and at 8 a.m. they reached the edge of the plain. Shirley decided to wait there until evening.

The patrol started off on the evening of Tuesday 6th and travelled north-west to try and cut the tracks of their outward journey. Four horses had already died and all the packs were abandoned, together with rifles and other gear. From that point on it must have been a trip through hell. The men struggled on through the night heat of November, with horses collapsing every mile. When there were only three left, Shirley, Giles and George Phillips rode on, leaving the last of the water with Hussey, Rees and Arthur Phillips, who would continue on foot. At around 1 o'clock on the morning of Wednesday 7th, the party's outward tracks were found. All the horses were by then dead. Giles sent one tracker ahead to bring back water and Shirley sent the other Aborigine on the same mission.

Giles thought they were still about 14 miles (22 kilometres) from Rees's well. Giles, Shirley and George Phillips struggled on along the tracks on foot.

Giles managed to go on a little way before collapsing under a small bush. He saw no sign of the others and later had little recollection of that day. In the evening he recovered a little and went on about 3 miles (5 kilometres). Hearing a voice, he discovered Shirley under the shelter of a small bush. Shirley was in a bad way. He told Giles that he thought George Phillips was lying dead about 300 metres back. Neither of them had the energy to check. While they were discussing the situation, they heard a faint cooee, and Hussey limped over and joined them; he had been camped close by during the heat of the day. All three men were close to complete exhaustion, and tormented by a terrible thirst. Shirley said he was unable to continue and no amount of encouragement could persuade him to rise. Giles and Hussey shook hands with him and struggled on towards the well, still 11 miles (17 kilometres) away.

Early next morning Giles could see timber about 2 miles (3 kilometres) ahead. Hussey, however, had collapsed and could go no further. Giles made it to the scrub line at about 6 a.m. and there lost consciousness. He came to as the tracker poured water over his head and face. After a drink, he and the tracker faced the last stage into Rees's well. Two miles from the water Giles had to stop and rest. He finally made it into camp at 5 p.m. on Thursday 8 November. It was just five days since he had ridden out from there with the patrol.

Giles had another drink, a wash and a sleep. At 1 o'clock on Friday morning he and the tracker took water back to try and save Hussey and Shirley. Five miles (8 kilometres) out from the well they both could go no further, and after cooeeing without any answer, they returned to the well. At 2 o'clock on Saturday morning Giles and the tracker started out for Attack Creek. They made it in three days. On Tuesday 13 November the wires of the Overland Telegraph Line ran hot with the news of the disaster. Five white men and one tracker had died of thirst. Ironically Redford and his party got to Corella with no difficulty.

It is easy to be wise after the event; however, if Giles's report is to be believed, then the unfortunate Mounted Constable Shirley should never have been in charge of the patrol. The causes that contributed to the debacle are obvious. The water carried by the patrol was inadequate for a party of eight, and more importantly, Shirley was a poor bushman who had little idea of how to cross a dry stage. To have travelled only 100 kilometres in two days and a night in country without water for horses was to invite disaster. As mentioned above, the leader of the patrol wasted hours of valuable travelling time on the second afternoon in a futile effort to find local water. Had he gone on, the patrol would have reached Corella the next day. Instead, with the bulk of the dry stage already behind him, Shirley decided to go back. It was the wrong decision, made worse by his poor navigation that night.

It may be said that having to follow Redford's tracks slowed the progress of the patrol. Perhaps, but that is not hard country. Even after two months had elapsed, any reasonable tracker should have been able to track a mounted party. It was a black week in the annals of the developing Territory, and a stern and early warning that the Barkly suffered fools not at all.

Some 65 years after the death of the six men, the remains of a saddle and two stirrup irons were found on Rockhampton Downs. I believe that Cecil Teece, who was head stockman there at the time, still has one of the irons in his possession. It is almost certain that these relics were part of the gear used by the ill-fated police patrol.

By the 1890s there were a number of cattle stations established on the Tableland. They were dependent, however, on surface water that was not always reliable. In January 1893 an early pioneer of the Tableland named David McKay died of thirst on a dry stretch between Alroy Downs and Brunette. His body was found some 25 kilometres from water. All his horses were dead, and he left a will in the form of a letter to the manager of Brunette.

The turn of the century brought a lengthy drought to the Territory. The Katherine to Anthony's Lagoon mailman, a man named Stibe, perished together with another white man named Hehir and an Aboriginal woman on this treacherous mail run. Harry Redford found the bodies beside holes they had dug with their bare hands.

The waterless stage across the Tableland, from Renner Springs to Eva Downs, was over 100 kilometres, with the only water available at Eva being from a well containing brackish water. To raise this water to the surface, the mailman had to manually work an ancient windlass. I have never tasted water from this well myself, but Alf Chambers told me that the well never improved and was still brackish until abandoned.

The last stage of the mail run was from Eva Downs to Anthony's Lagoon. This stage, although shorter, is just as dry. It was on this leg that Stibe and his companions died of thirst. This hazardous mail service was done by packhorse eight times a year. No wonder the 'Fizzer', who took it on after Stibe's death, was in fear of perishing.

In *Frontier Country*, Glenville Pike tells of another party that perished in January 1902. Four men left Powell's Creek to go to Anthony's Lagoon. The party was travelling in a four-in-hand buckboard, and took along spare horses. The men appear to have strayed off the mailman's track, which is not surprising, for it would not be all that well defined. They were reported missing, and a police search found the vehicle and perished horses about 50 kilometres south of the mail road. The bodies of the men were found some weeks later.

Two drovers, a father and son named Hopkins, perished on the western side of the Rankine River only 6 miles (10 kilometres) out from Shady Camp, a good waterhole that is known to drovers. There is a bit of a mystery about the deaths of the Hopkins. They were drovers and presumably reasonably good bushmen. They must have known the river was east of them, yet when less than 10 kilometres from water, they cut their horses' throats to assuage their thirst—and perished. I have heard rumours that the Hopkins may have been the victims of foul play, and that their deaths were made to look as though they had perished from thirst. It is said they had not long before been paid for the delivery of cattle.

There have been others, too, men who have died horrible deaths alone. A pumper on Alexandria rode away to his death when Jimmy Fowler was running the camp there. Pumpers were employed to look after the diesel engines that drove the pump heads on the sub-artesian bores. This chap's name was Robinson. He had a horse plant at the bore he was looking after, and it is thought he got slewed, lost, looking for horses that had strayed. Despite a prolonged search by Fowler and others, Robinson's body was never found. Another pumper perished on Gallipoli, an outstation of Alexandria. He walked away from the bore in very hot weather when the manager was absent in Camooweal. It was a tragedy that many thought should not have happened.

One man I knew only as 'Spinifex' perished when he was almost in sight of the Georgina River. He was bringing a plant of horses up the river to Camooweal at the end of the year. It is believed Spinifex had been on the grog at Urandangie and this may have contributed to him becoming disorientated. The two big factors in this kind of death are panic and disorientation. Panic prevents clear thinking, and adds to the feeling of disorientation. People who have become lost and disorientated have been known to do crazy things. Their tracks have shown that they have ridden or walked over roads or creeks, and have even climbed through fences, without appearing to realise that each of these could provide a path to safety.

During the 1940s two double tragedies occurred on Rockhampton Downs in the heart of the Barkly Tableland. In the first, which shocked the Territory, a young doctor named Straede, from Tennant Creek, perished together with his wife while travelling on the station to attend a sick woman there. The train of circumstances that led to the double tragedy was a direct result of wartime measures.

Among the evacuees from Darwin after the bombing was a Mrs Jones. Her sons had been at boarding school with the Easey lads from Rockhampton Downs and had spent the school holidays as guests of the manager, George Easey, and his wife. It was natural, then, that Mrs Jones chose to visit the station when she was evacuated. Mrs Jones, however, was suffering from a duodenal ulcer. During her stay at Rockhampton Downs, she haemorrhaged badly and was in urgent need of medical attention. The flying doctor base at Cloncurry was contacted, but there was no plane available: the Qantas planes used by the flying doctor service had been pressed into coastal surveillance duties. Neither Rockhampton Downs nor Cloncurry had direct phone contact with Tennant Creek, the nearest hospital, so the call virtually had to travel around Australia for medical help to be reached.

Dr Straede set out in the afternoon to drive to Rockhampton Downs, taking his young wife with him. The doctor had little or no experience in the bush; however, he did take a 1 gallon (4½ litres) container of water with him. The pair never arrived at Rockhampton Downs.

Due to the torturous nature of communications, George Easey was not aware that the pair was overdue until the afternoon of the next day. He immediately set out in a utility truck, taking his young son Ron with him. The road to Rockhampton Downs ran past a station watering facility named No. 3 bore. The tracks of the doctor's car were not picked up until they were identified arriving at this bore. A large number of cattle were watering there and for a distance of over a kilometre out from the bore the road was obliterated by cattle pads.

After some trouble, they picked up the tracks of the doctor's car leaving the bore. Then began the difficult task of tracking it through the tall grass and rough going. The manager drove while his keen-eyed son stood on the running board and directed his father. A number of times the tracks were lost, but finally, just on sundown, the searchers found the doctor's small English model car. It had a broken petrol pipe.

It was with dismay that George and his son saw the tracks of the doctor and his wife walking away from the vehicle towards No. 3 bore. The tracks were at least 24 hours old and it was getting too dark to attempt to follow them. In any case, as the pair had not reached the bore, George believed it would have been futile. It was apparent to him that the pair had already perished. He decided to return to the station and organise a search the following day.

The authorities in Tennant Creek had been notified at the same time as George Easey. That night the police, plus a friend of the missing pair, arrived at the station. At daylight next morning a full scale search was organised, and Aboriginal trackers found the bodies of the doctor and his wife late that morning. They died three kilometres from water at No. 3 bore.

The tracks told the sorry story of the tragedy. Having failed to find the road where it left No. 3 bore, the young doctor headed off in an effort to try and find it. The going was exceedingly rough, with large tussocks of bull mitchell grass and potholes. Doctor Straede drove around in a desperate attempt to pick up the road, but instead of circling back to the bore when he failed to find the road, he drove off in an almost straight line to the north.

It must have been a sickening blow to the young couple when the car's engine stopped. The petrol pipe had snapped, marooning the pair 12 kilometres from the bore they had left earlier. Due to ignorance of bush lore, the unfortunate pair then broke the fundamental rule of survival. They walked away from the vehicle. By then it would have been late afternoon, but it was February and the temperature on the open downs would have been still in the forties. They never stood a chance.

It was a tragedy that would have been averted had they stayed with the vehicle instead of panicking and walking off. There was drinkable water in the radiator of the car, and it would have been cool by the time the water they carried was exhausted. This was adequate, had they remained calm, to last them until rescued. Ironically, there was another station bore under five kilometres from where the car had broken down—its sails could be seen through the trees on a supplejack ridge.

The doctor and his wife were buried in Tennant Creek. Mrs Jones was finally airlifted from Rockhampton Downs, but the unfortunate woman died later in the Brisbane Hospital.

I spoke to Ron Easey about the tragedy. It is almost 47 years since Dr Straede and his wife perished, but Ron's memory of the events are still clear and concise. He believes this is because of his age at the time, and the magnitude of the tragedy.

Towards the end of 1949 Rockhampton Downs saw another double tragedy. The Aboriginal women from the homestead decided to go on walkabout, taking with them two young girls of the tribe. The girls were sisters. Londa, the oldest, was about 14 years of age and her sister was a few years younger. The Aborigines expected to find water in a native well or waterhole they knew. When they arrived there, though, there was nothing but dried mud. Ignoring this warning, the party decided to go on further to another well where they were confident they would find water. Their confidence was misplaced, however, for there was no water at the second well either. The party was now in a parlous situation. It was midsummer and the sun blazed down unmercifully on the scorched earth. The only chance the women had was to make it back to the station bore they had left on their inadvisable excursion.

The women found the going difficult enough, but for the two young girls it was just too much. When the youngest could go no further, she was left beside a wild orange bush. The bush was laden with fruit, but the wild orange does little to assuage thirst. The rest of the party struggled on, the women hoping to get the older girl to the bore. It was futile, however. Londa collapsed less than two kilometres from water and by the time the older women returned with some, she was dead.

Possibly because they felt responsible, the women seemed loath to tell what had happened to the two missing girls. When it was finally established that the girls had probably perished, George Easey, the manager, organised a search party and set out to find the bodies. The body of the oldest girl was found first, and later that of her younger sister. The Tennant Creek police were notified and a constable arrived two days later, together with an official from the Aboriginal settlement at Phillip

Creek. The bodies, which had not been disturbed, were inspected and buried where they were found.

I was working in the Gulf when the tragedy occurred. Cecil Teece, who I had known quite well in the Territory, told me about it later. Although some years had passed, I could see that he felt deeply about the tragedy. At the time, he was head stockman on Rockhampton Downs and had a young family himself. Londa had helped his wife with the children.

Peter Treloar, who was jackarooing on Rockhampton Downs when the tragedy occurred, was a member of both the search and the burial party. I met Peter under quite different circumstances. Ray Drummond, a friend of mine at Caboolture, asked me if I would like to help with a bit of branding. I jumped at the chance and we went up to a small cattle place on Delaney Creek. The place was owned by a mate of his, and the mate turned out to be Peter Treloar. After the branding was done, we repaired to the homestead verandah for a cold stubby. As we had all worked on cattle properties, the talk soon turned to cattle. Peter mentioned Rockhampton Downs and I asked him if he knew anything about the girls' deaths. He nodded, passed me another cold one and told me of his involvement as a young jackaroo.

Peter also told me of the narrow escape of a head stockman on Rockhampton Downs before Cecil Teece took over the camp. This chap came very close to perishing when he became lost. He was found in a very bad way, stark naked and burnt almost black by the sun. The shedding of clothing is a common phenomenon in cases where Europeans are almost at the point of dying of thirst.

Most of the people who perished on the Barkly Tableland were adults, and many were bushmen. It was an area that earned its sinister reputation, for it seldom gave a person a second chance.

The Tank

In the blazing summer of 'eighty-one,
A musterer vanished from Mulga run;
'Twas a tragic story, an oft-told one
  Then in the further out.
They found the spot where his stockhorse died,
With a twisted leg in a hole beside;
But to track the rider in vain they tried;
  He perished without a doubt.

Thirst-crazed and limping, his stockhorse gone,
With senses reeling he staggered on,
Mocked by a phantom lake that shone,
  Where a rough ridge met the plain.
Keep going, keep going, his fevered mind
Urged, keep going you've got to find
Water ahead, there is death behind;
  And the mirage gleamed again.

And then as the rough ridge veered askance,
As the heat waves whirled in a fiendish dance,
He staked his all on that final chance,
  And, losing, he had to pay.
For then, as always, the mirage lied,
There was nought but mud that was cracked and dried,
In a shallow creek by the ridge's side;
  Then sobbing he crawled away.

With bleeding fingers he tore the ground,
Where the twisted roots of the gidgee wound,
But there wasn't water the stockman found,
  Where the age-old ridges wait.
And the dingoes knew as they slunk close by,
While the black crows mocked at his strangled cry,
With ghoulish interest they watched him die,
  Lest they, too, should be tricked by Fate.

Out there on the black-soil plain today,
Where heat waves shimmer and whirlwinds play,
Mirages beckon and show the way,
  To water beside the hill.
And a man might follow it eager eyed,
With dry lips swollen and stumbling stride,
Not seeing the figure in step beside,
  To splash there and drink his fill.

For they came to the spot where the stockman prayed,
O'er a dusty hole that his hands had made;
And there with tractor and scoop and blade,
  They threw up a giant tank.
The ridge top crowned in dusty wreath,
Flung back the echoes as gleaming teeth
Tore down to the virgin clay beneath,
  By the side of the growing bank.

Unknowing they raised ere they went their way,
An incongrous monument formed of clay,
A rippling gem in a glasp of grey,
  It stands by the gidgee hill.

Where the Pelican Builds

The horses were ready, the rails were down,
  But the riders lingered still—
One had a parting word to say,
  And one had his pipe to fill.
Then they mounted, one with a granted prayer,
  And one would with a grief unguessed.
'We are going,' they said as they rode away,
  'Where the pelican builds her nest!'

They had told us of pastures wide and green,
  To be sought past the sunset's glow;
Of rifts in the ranges by opal lit,
  And gold 'neath the river's flow.
And thirst and hunger were banished words
  When they spoke of the unknown West;
No drought they dreaded, no flood they feared,
  Where the pelican builds her nest!

The creek at the ford was but fetlock deep
  When we watched them crossing there;
The rains have replenished it thrice since then,
  And thrice has the rock lain bare.
But the waters of Hope have flowed and fled,
  And never from blue hill's breast
Come back—by the sun and the sands devoured—
  Where the pelican builds her nest!

Mary Hannay Foott

Where the Pelican Builds

During the first half of the last century opinions regarding the centre of our continent differed widely. Many believed it held an inland sea; others, including some men of note, believed it to be a well-watered region, a veritable land of milk and honey, where that ubiquitous bird, the pelican, built its nest. This opinion persisted despite the reports of explorers Edward John Eyre and Charles Sturt. The journeys of John McDouall Stuart in 1861–62 bisected the continent from south to north and his reports did a lot to dispel the fanciful ideas of an inland utopia. In the 1870s Ernest Giles, John Warburton and John Forrest explored west from the centre, while Frank Scarr and W.O. Hodgkinson travelled west from the limits of settlement in Queensland. These expeditions finally wrote finis to the dream of an inland paradise.

In 1877 a trio led by the redoubtable Nat Buchanan travelled from the Buchanan Creek to Attack Creek, then on to Powell's Creek. It was an outstanding feat. On the way from the lower Buchanan to Attack Creek, the party discovered the lake system into which most of the Barkly Tableland streams flow. Surrounded by blue bush and coolabahs, it was a poor substitute for an inland sea, but the closest to it anyone was to find.

Mary Hannay Foott wrote the touching poem 'Where the Pelican Builds'. It was published in her anthology *The Wide Brown Land* in 1885. The verses clearly illustrate the earlier held belief of there being a fertile inland region. Mary was a Scottish lass who came to this country as a child. She later married a grazier named Foott who took up a run he called Dundoo on Yowah Creek, south-west of Charleville.

Mary Hannay Foott's poem may well have been written about the Prout brothers, who disappeared west of the Georgina early in 1878. Mary may have met them; she certainly would have heard of their failure to return.

Coming as it did just 30 years after Leichhardt's disappearance, the fate of Sydney (Cornelius) and Albert Prout was the subject of great debate throughout Queensland. In some reports the elder brother is referred to as Sydney and in others, as Cornelius; I shall refer to him as Cornelius throughout. Cornelius and Albert were the sons of Lieutenant

Cornelius Prout. The boys' father came to the colony as an officer on the HMS *Warspite*. He left the navy and took up a senior job in the administration of the infant colony. Both his sons were born in Sydney and received the best education possible, growing up as accepted members of Sydney society. Although they had little knowledge of the bush, they both had ambitions of becoming graziers so, purchasing a small herd of young cows and some herd bulls, they set out for Queensland to establish a station.

The Prouts, however, had left it too late. The further they went, the more disillusioned they became. The country had all been taken up. In the late 1860s and early 1870s settlement in Queensland had spread west and north like wildfire. In 1875–76 when W.O. Hodgkinson led an expedition to explore the country between the Diamantina River and the Northern Territory border, a great deal of the area had already been taken up, for the squatters had outstripped exploration on much of the frontier.

In 1877 the Prouts finally arrived at King Creek, a tributary of the Georgina. There they settled on a small block south-west of Boulia. The block on King Creek was not the grand station that the Prout brothers had dreamed of and Cornelius and Albert decided to search further out. Leaving the run, they rode out to the Mulligan River. Beyond the Mulligan was semi-desert populated by unfriendly Aborigines, but at Lake Amaroo, just west of the Mulligan, Herbert Downs had established an outstation. Bitterly disappointed, the Prout brothers returned to their small holding. But the dream of owning a large station still inspired the two brothers.

They decided they would have to go further out past the Georgina and the Mulligan and there, perhaps, they would find what they wanted. When news of Nat Buchanan's successful journey reached the Prouts later in 1877, it may well have motivated them to action. On 2 December 1877 the Prout brothers set out westwards. With them was a white stockman named Baker and an Aborigine from the Diamantina area. They took a plant of more than 20 horses, with adequate rations for some months. They were possibly trying to emulate Nat Buchanan, to find unknown pastoral areas and to establish a route through to the Overland Telegraph Line. However, none of the party had the skills and the experience of Buchanan. Moreover, it was far too late in the year to attempt such a journey. The heat out there in December is a killer. None of the party ever returned.

William Henry James Carr-Boyd was with Hodgkinson's expedition of 1875–76. A commanding figure of a man with a huge appetite for life and a well-developed liking for rum, Carr-Boyd was an adventurer who revelled in life on the frontier. He had a fine voice, was a renowned campfire raconteur and wrote to the Southern papers using the nom de plume of 'Potjostler'. Above all else, Carr-Boyd was an excellent bushman.

In 1878 Carr-Boyd was at Amaroo helping in the search for a missing man named Greensmith, who had apparently been murdered by Aborigines. When he heard that the Prouts were missing, he wrote to the *Queenslander*, stating that they would be found 140 miles (approximately 225 kilometres) west of Amaroo. He added that for £1000 he would find them if it was at all possible. He stated that he had earlier met 'Sydney' Prout and Baker and advised them to head for Mount Harriet, some 40 miles (64 kilometres) north-west of Amaroo. He also told them where to find water. Mount Harriet is one of two peaks known as twin hills; its sister peak is Mount Kate. There is a waterhole south of the hills named Marked Tree waterhole, which should not be confused with Mark Tree hole on the Georgina. The tree near the twin hills could have been

Ruins of Amaroo Outstation. Photo: Ian Tinney

marked by Hodgkinson, and no doubt Carr-Boyd knew the area. Carr-Boyd added that he had found a camp of the party's en route to Mount Harriet.

The disappearance of the Prout brothers caused general concern among the settlers of far western Queensland. In mid-1878 Frank Scarr, a surveyor, and an official with the Queensland Crown Lands Department, led an expedition to establish a route from the Georgina to the Overland Telegraph Line. In his first unsuccessful attempt, he travelled up Pituri Creek, a tributary of the Georgina. At a waterhole approximately 100 miles (160 kilometres) up Pituri Creek, he found evidence of the Prout party. The waterhole is in Manners Creek, a tributary of Pituri Creek.

According to Scarr, it lies approximately 22 degrees 17 minutes south and 137 degrees 40 minutes east. At the waterhole Scarr found a pair of moleskins split up the legs, stained with what looked like blood. He also found a shirt still twisted as though it was being wrung out when dropped. Several bits of a blue blanket, bits of calico and pieces of a felt hat were picked up as well. While he was there, horses came in to water. They had badly marked backs, as though they had been running free while saddled. According to Scarr, it appeared that the saddles had slipped under the horses' bellies and the girths had cut into their backs. These horses were branded C6P and were later identified as belonging to the missing party. Scarr, who obviously had little time for Aborigines, believed that the whites had been surprised and killed. He stated that he thought the 'natives' had eaten the bodies, and later had either burnt the bones or had carried them away.

Scarr then proceeded on his original mission, but was forced back and turned east to the Georgina. He later won through to Tennant Creek on a more northerly route.

Late in 1878 an agreement was reached between Carr-Boyd and Mr P. McGuigan, of Davenport Downs. Carr-Boyd was commissioned to search for the Prouts. The Prouts and Baker had been missing for a little over 12 months—they had expected to return within three months of leaving King Creek. According to Carr-Boyd, McGuigan would have initiated the search earlier but for the presence of two native police patrols in the area. He had expected them to undertake the task. A situation resembling guerilla warfare existed at that time on the Queensland frontier. The same month Carr-Boyd and McGuigan met, a settler named Molvo and his party had been wiped out north of Boulia. Earlier a station hand, Greensmith, had been killed out from Amaroo and James McCromarky, a station manager, had been speared to death at an outstation on the Diamantina. There were, of course, others.

The agreement between Carr-Boyd and P. McGuigan was signed on 29 December 1878 at Davenport Station. For his part, Carr-Boyd was to undertake a seven week search for the Prouts, taking with him one white man and 10 horses. What McGuigan's commitment was Carr-Boyd never spelt out—it may have been the £1000 he had nominated earlier.

Carr-Boyd ignored the condition regarding the white man. He selected instead, John Stokes, an Aborigine. Also with him was another Aborigine named Davey who acted as interpreter. Carr-Boyd wrote in his report that Stokes was reliable and one of the best bushmen he knew, and that he had been with Scarr. Carr-Boyd was quick to point out, however, that the success of the venture was due to him, not Stokes. Carr-Boyd was not renowned for his modesty and he, of course, wrote the report, a significant advantage, as most people would know.

The trip did not get off to a good start. Obtaining the horses proved to be a real headache and valuable time was lost. Carr-Boyd had left Davenport with an authority from McGuigan to pick up 10 horses belonging to the Prouts. These horses were running on an outstation of Glengyle west of the Georgina which was managed by a man called Colvin. The outstation was probably Sandringham. Colvin refused to hand over the horses, telling Carr-Boyd he would have to go to the head station and get permission from Campbell, the manager. Carr-Boyd rode down the river to Glengyle to find Campbell absent and the relieving manager as recalcitrant as Colvin.

Finally Carr-Boyd did obtain three horses from Colvin and another two from a man called McHatter. Carr-Boyd helped him rescue two station boys kidnapped by a group of some 200 Aborigines. He then set out with six horses and headed for Pituri Creek. At Idamea (Glenormiston) he obtained another horse plus a gun and rations. He left there with seven horses, John Stokes and two other Aborigines.

At the end of the first day's travelling Carr-Boyd camped at Lake Wanditta, which he described as being over three kilometres long by almost one kilometre wide. About 100 Aborigines were also camped there and next morning Carr-Boyd rounded them up and interrogated them. He wanted to know two things: was there any water further up the creek, and did they know anything of the missing party. Davey

Lake Wanditta in a dry season. Photo: Lloyd Lindon-Smith

advised Carr-Boyd that according to the Aborigines there was no water at all up Pituri Creek, and that they had heard white men had been killed up there, but there was no water at the place. Carr-Boyd knew from past experience that there was water 110 kilometres further up in Manners Creek, a tributary of Pituri, and decided further questioning was futile. Carr-Boyd always referred to Pituri Creek and its main tributary as Manners Creek.

Pituri Creek is on Glenormiston Station. In 1947–48 I worked there as a stockman. On a number of occasions during that time I was involved in musters along Pituri Creek and around Lake Wanditta. The lake was not then the pristine body of water seen by Carr-Boyd. Cloven-footed animals have a disastrous effect on the fragile top soil of the inland; silting caused by 70 years of cattle grazing had reduced the capacity of Lake Wanditta. In 1947–48 no Aborigines fished or gathered mussels there—no campfires glowed along the banks and no corroborees echoed across the silent water from the fringing coolabahs. I found plenty of evidence of past tenure, but the proud Wonkajerras, custodians of the Pituri tree, had vanished, leaving behind neither kith nor kin.

Before he left Wanditta, Carr-Boyd persuaded an Aboriginal youth to accompany him. How gentle the persuasion is left to the imagination.

Carr-Boyd put him on a packhorse and drove him along with the horses. Three miles (5 kilometres) from the camp the party saw a creek, which Carr-Boyd describes as coming in from the south-west. In his report he said this was Kelly's Creek. He was obviously wrong about this, unless names have changed, for it could only have been Linda Creek. To say it came in from the south-west is a bit puzzling; however, he ran the creek up for 50 kilometres and would have seen its course higher up.

Carr-Boyd's decision to go up Linda Creek was fortunate. On the return journey he found Pituri Creek dry for 80 kilometres above the junction with Linda Creek. Some 16 kilometres up Linda Creek they came to a good waterhole. Another 10 kilometres up was another smaller hole. Here Carr-Boyd decided to dismiss his Aboriginal guide, who he said in his report was full of humbug. The party then travelled another 24 kilometres and camped at a fine waterhole. Next day Carr-Boyd struck out to the north-west and, after travelling 50 kilometres, arrived at a hole in Manners Creek where both Hodgkinson and Scarr had previously camped.

The following day another 50 kilometres brought them to the waterhole where Scarr had found the horses and other evidence of the Prouts' presence. Carr-Boyd searched the area and found a packsaddle near the hole, but found nothing of the clothing and blanket mentioned by Scarr. Carr-Boyd also found a marked tree with the following cut into it: '25/7/78' over 'F. SCARR' over '111' over 'WHITES MURDERED' over '5 HORSES C6P' over 'GOT SUPP' over 'PARTY'. Carr-Boyd then cut his own mark in the tree. It must have been a very big tree.

At this point in his report Carr-Boyd wrote that no explorer need have any fear of the blacks in the area. The secret, he added, was knowing how to deal with them, but did not elaborate. As it seemed obvious that the Prouts had been killed or had perished, Carr-Boyd was keen to obtain help from the local tribe in locating their remains. As no Aborigines came to the waterhole, he set out alone in a westerly direction to find either another creek or to contact 'natives'. He was unsuccessful on both counts and returned to camp. The next day Carr-Boyd sent John Stokes and one of his boys down Manners Creek to see if they could make contact with a tribal group they had seen on the way to their present camp. Stokes came back with the news that a large group had camped eight kilometres down the creek the night before, but had gone before they arrived. Their tracks led off in a westerly direction. Stokes followed the tracks for

16 kilometres—they came quite close to Carr-Boyd's camp—then Stokes returned.

Next morning Carr-Boyd packed up and set out to track the Aborigines. Picking the tracks up where Stokes had left them, the party travelled another 16 kilometres in a west-south-west direction. They then saw two old Aboriginal women gathering nardoo on the downs. A line of timber was not far off and the women made for this to join the rest of the tribe. Carr-Boyd rounded up the old women, let the rest go, and made a temporary camp for a meal. When questioned, the two women did nothing but yell and howl; Carr-Boyd then let one go and concentrated on the other. Finally she admitted through Davey that she knew of a place where white man's bones were, together with saddles and clothes. It was, she said, a long way away and laughed at the idea of the party getting there that night.

Carr-Boyd was getting short of rations and was keen to get the business over. He packed up, and put the woman on a horse. She led them due west, and after they had travelled 45 kilometres, the downs ended and they came to a gorge. Carr-Boyd described this as being very pretty. The party went up a creek in the gorge and after four kilometres came to a waterhole. Carr-Boyd wrote that this water was about the worst he had ever tasted. As it was by this time almost dark, they made camp. The old Aboriginal woman told them that the site where the remains were was not far off.

Next morning Davey told Carr-Boyd that the old woman knew nothing of white man's bones. She had, he said, led them away so the tribe would not be harmed. Carr-Boyd advised her through Davey that if she did not show them the place, he would wipe out the tribe. John Stokes believed that Davey was the problem. He raced at the interpreter with a spear and, grabbing him by the throat, threatened to kill him unless he spoke the truth. Davey saw the light and the old woman led the party on. According to Carr-Boyd, they had only travelled some 5 kilometres up a blue bush flat when he spotted the remains of a camp over to his right. On investigation, the skeletal remains of Cornelius Prout, together with those of a horse, were found. Two packsaddles and packbags, a riding saddle and various camp equipment were scattered about, as well as a blackened billy can that had the words 'no water yet' scratched on it. Among the scattered gear were items identified as belonging to A.E. Prout, and a letter addressed to Albert Prout from his mother. It appeared that a bushfire had been over the camp. Carr-Boyd also found a tattered diary with the last entry dated 26 January 1878, less than two months since starting out.

From the diary, Carr-Boyd gleaned that the Prouts had travelled through a great deal of country previously unknown to whites. Apparently they had been travelling due east for two days trying to get back to Manners Creek. Baker had been there twice before, but the Prouts must have turned south-east and travelled 30 kilometres along a blue bush flat that ran almost parallel with Manners Creek, when they were, in fact, no more than that distance from the creek itself. It had, according to Carr-Boyd, been a fatal mistake. He reconstructed the tragedy as follows. With most of the horses knocked up, Cornelius Prout had stayed at the camp while Baker, and his brother (Carr-Boyd does not mention the Aborigine who was with them) went to look for water. The pair then made another mistake by turning south instead of following the flat down to the creek in the gorge. Carr-Boyd does not say whether he gained this information by following tracks, or by deduction. Had they continued on down the flat, he claimed, they would have reached the hole in Manners Creek within 50 kilometres.

Cornelius Prout's body was identified by its size and a dint in the skull from a previous accident. As Carr-Boyd found no evidence of attack by Aborigines, it appears that Cornelius died of thirst while waiting vainly for the others to bring back water. He must have gone through absolute hell. Few people can imagine the torment of thirst and despair he would have endured before death claimed him.

Carr-Boyd spent half a day vainly searching for Albert Prout and Baker. The Aboriginal woman took him to a creek where she said the bones of two white men had been burned. Carr-Boyd took this creek to be part of Kelly's Creek. As rations had just about run out and the water was foul, he stayed no longer. Carr-Boyd gathered the remains of the elder Prout with most of the personal items and started back to Manners Creek. He reached Idamea in three days, and eight days later Carr-Boyd delivered Cornelius Prout's remains to Mr McGuigan at Davenport Downs as per the agreement.

Carr-Boyd's description of distances travelled and his direction of travel may cause some confusion; for instance, after cutting the tracks out from the camp at Manners Creek, he travelled a total of 70 kilometres to the death site, yet wrote that it was only 50 kilometres back to the waterhole. The discrepancy may be explained by the route taken to get to the site, and by the fact that distance between points was calculated by time travelled multiplied by the estimated rate of progress per hour.

On Carr-Boyd's return, the mystery of the Prout brothers disappearance had been solved, it seemed, but a lot of unanswered questions remained. Did Albert Prout and Baker die of thirst or were they killed by Aborigines? Was the Aboriginal woman telling the truth about the remains on Kelly's Creek? How did the saddle-marked horses get to the waterhole in Manners Creek? Who was disturbed while wringing out the shirt Scarr found? Did Baker and Albert Prout get to that waterhole, or was it only one of them?

It may seem futile to attempt to answer those questions, yet if the known facts are analysed objectively a clearer picture may emerge:

1. No known white men had been in the area of Manners Creek since Hodgkinson's expedition.
2. The horses at the hole in Manners Creek definitely belonged to the Prout brothers.
3. Two packs were found at the death scene; the Prouts would have had more. A pack was found by Carr-Boyd at the waterhole.
4. According to the diary found by Carr-Boyd, the Prouts had been trying to reach Manners Creek.
5. A partly wrung-out shirt was found at the waterhole by Scarr, together with scraps of blanket and a pair of moleskin trousers stained with what appeared to Scarr to be blood.
6. Scarr stated that the horses' backs were badly saddle marked, as if the saddles had rolled and been that way for some time.

Conclusion: 1. Some of the Prout party did reach the waterhole, and 2. A white man, or white men, had been surprised there and possibly killed by Aborigines in the vicinity.

The country west of Pituri Creek is fairly inhospitable, but Baker was a good bushman who had been in the area before. On the evidence, then, Baker or Albert Prout, or both of them, did reach the waterhole in Manners Creek. If this is so, however, his or their behaviour there raises other questions. Why would anyone spend precious time in washing a shirt when a man dying of thirst was dependent on having water taken back to him?

Here we must abandon fact and rely purely on speculation. A possible explanation could be that the death of Cornelius Prout was already known to whoever was at the waterhole. One could speculate further on how this may have been known, but speculation is, at best, dangerous ground. The facts relating to the final chapter of the tragedy will never be known.

Rocky Creek

The rain swept down on the streaming bush as the lightning lit the road,
Where the big truck sped like a charging bull, head down with its two-tier load.
Young weaner steers from a basalt run en route to the southern sales,
A day and night on the Queensland roads then on into New South Wales.
The downpour lashed at the cabin glass and the wheel spray billowed wide
From the runoff water across the road that spread like a rising tide.

The lights of a township gleamed and neared through the wipers' frantic beat,
And the truckie eased on the brakes and stopped by the pub in the only street.
He checked his load in the driving rain, then ran from his big machine,
As he crossed the floor the barman saw he was built like a brick latrine.
He shook the rain from his shaggy head as he called for a pot of beer.
'It's nasty weather,' the barman said, 'are you thinking of camping here?'

'Just a couple of drinks,' the truckie said, 'and then I'll be on me way,
These weaners are wanted in New South Wales and I don't mean yesterday.
The rain won't worry this rig of mine, when I'm hauling a livestock load,
She'll plough through water a metre deep as long as there's still a road.'
'Then take it easy,' the barman said, 'when you get down to Rocky Creek,
It's been raining back in the ranges now for almost a flaming week.

'It's one of those creeks you can never trust, as most of the locals know,
The last of the packhorse mailmen drowned in a flood there years ago.
The mails were a sacred trust to him and a duty he'd never fail,
I've heard it said you could set your watch on time with the packhorse mail.
He lost his life on a night like this, he'd battled through miles of mud,
With never a qualm or a backward glance he tackled the Rocky flood.

'It was running a banker then, I'm told, and it swept with a sullen roar
As the mailman swam with the Royal Mail as often he'd done before.
He was halfway over the raging stream, the current was running strong,
When a tree came rolling down Rocky Creek as a flood crest swirled along.
The man and his horses had no chance, it was curtains for Tom McHugh,
He drowned upholding the service code: "The mail must be taken through."

'They say his ghost can be often seen when the stars wink cold and pale,
As he rides the reaches of Rocky Creek still trying to save the mail.'
The truckie grinned at the barman then. 'That's a damn good yarn, no sweat,
I've seen some sights on the flamin' road but a ghost I have never met.
Well, I'm out of here and I won't pull up 'till I meet with the morning light,
And I won't be swimming that flamin' creek, I will cross by the bridge tonight.'

The truckie settled behind the wheel for a night that would hold no sleep,
The miles slipped by and the rain eased off, but the gullies still ran deep.
The big rig cruised from the timbered ridge to the scrublands down below
As the truckie tapped on the steering wheel in time with the radio.
The airwaves carried a country song, on life 'neath the western sky,
When a man rode out of the scrub ahead with his right arm held on high.

The truckie gasped as he hit the brakes and sounded a warning blast,
But the horseman turned to the speeding truck, with the gap now closing fast.
The truckie cursed as he dropped a gear, then he dropped a cog again,
The gear box heaved as it took the load and it howled like a thing in pain.
He rode the brakes 'till the trailer slewed and some of the weaners fell,
But the man rode straight at the swaying truck like a horseman straight from hell.

With the trailer skidding behind the rig and a madman right ahead,
The truckie knew that all hope he had of avoiding a crash had fled.
He braced himself for the coming prang, but the high beam headlights shone
Through the ghostly face of a man long dead, then the rider and horse were gone.
The blood ran cold in the truckie's veins and the cold sweat wreathed his brow,
But he eased the brakes on the slowing truck and he kept control somehow.

He kept control with his mind awhirl. If the barman's tale was true,
Then the bearded rider who blocked his path was the spirit of Tom McHugh.
He drove on slowly around a bend, to be met with a chilling scene,
For a raging torrent in Rocky Creek roared past where the bridge had been.
He hit the brakes 'till the tyres planed, and he thought of his kids and wife,
And he prayed as the trailer jack-knifed round, for another chance in life.

The truck slid on as the truckie's hands froze stiff on the wheel with fright,
But the big rig stopped on the very brink with the trailer still upright.
The truckie looked at the cold grey flood that almost had been his shroud,
Then his head dropped onto the steering wheel and the big man sobbed aloud.
He landed down at the sales at last though he got there three days late,
And well he knew he'd been guided there by more than the hand of fate.

He may have imagined the ghost, he owns, for hallucinations can
Play wilful tricks in the dead of night on the mind of a weary man.
He stays down south of the border now, but at times he will quietly speak
Of the fateful night when his big rig stopped by the torrent in Rocky Creek—
How he fought the wheel as the tyres planed and he cursed at his slewing load
When the ghost of a mailman saved his life in the rain on a northern road.

Dangerous Waters

I reined the grey mare up at the bank of the channel. It would be a swim, I knew, but not a difficult one. It was still water, but still or dead water can be more treacherous at times than a strong current. If you swim diagonally across a running stream, the current can help to pull you across, but in dead water the swimmer has to depend entirely on his own efforts. I had every confidence in the mare, however, as I had been swimming her over many such channels for the past week or so and she had demonstrated she was a steady and reliable mare in water.

As in most situations, familiarity breeds contempt, and I put the mare into the water without stripping off my clothing, an omission that has proved critical in many swimming fatalities. The mare negotiated the swim quite well, but on facing the opposite bank she panicked and reared over backwards. I failed to get completely clear and found myself pinned to the bottom with the mare across my legs. She struggled and, in getting up, struck me a heavy blow on the shoulder with one hoof.

When I finally managed to reach the surface, my lungs were bursting, and I crawled up the bank to where my bedraggled mount was standing. The mare's legs were trembling and so were mine, for I realised just how close I had come to drowning. Had the mare struck me on the head rather than on the shoulder, I would have still been at the bottom of the channel.

Two very well known characters in the Northern Territory met their death by drowning. Henry Peckham, the 'Fizzer' of *We of the Never Never* fame, was drowned in the Victoria River in April 1911 and well-known cattle duffer Harry Redford, or Readford, drowned at Corella waterhole on Brunette Downs in the Northern Territory on 12 March 1901. Peckham was doing his first trip on the Katherine to Victoria River Downs mail run. Earlier he had been the mailman on the notorious Katherine to Anthony Lagoon run, a hazardous trip on which death from thirst was a constant threat. Peckham had a terror of perishing in this way, so it is ironic that he met his death in water. The Fizzer was buried at the crossing where he drowned. Later his body was removed and buried in the Elsey Cemetery.

Harry Redford won dubious fame as the man who stole the mob of cattle from Mount Cornish Station near Longreach and drove them to

The grave of the 'Fizzer' at the Elsey Cemetery. Photo: Ian Tinney

Harry Redford's grave at Corella Creek. Photo: Ted Egan

South Australia. At his trial the jury must have considered the feat to be greater than the crime, for they failed to convict him. The theft was immortalised in the book *Robbery Under Arms* by Rolf Boldrewood. Redford's swag and gear, minus a bridle, was found at Corella waterhole by James Hutton on 13 March, the day after he had drowned. On the 14th Harry Redford's naked body was found in the water. He had apparently drowned while swimming across to get his horses; perhaps he got tangled in the bridle. His grave is beside the creek, while the remains of his homestead lie on the low ridge beyond.

Almost all drownings in inland waters have occurred while men have been on the job, or as a result of unexpectedly high floods generated by unusually high rainfall. In late December 1916 and early January 1917 torrential rain fell in Queensland. The ensuing floods resulted in fatalities from the Gulf Country to Clermont, a bush town situated approximately 160 kilometres north-west of Rockhampton. Thomas Humphries, an eighteen year old stockman, was drowned while crossing the Gilbert River on horseback. The Gilbert was just one of the northern streams that rose to record heights in the 1916–1917 floods. Gerado Daimaz, a surveyor's offsider, was swept to his death by the Gilliat River. Torrential rain over

The author and Eugene Costin at the grave of Harry Redford. Photo: Ted Egan

four days at Mount Emu sent floods roaring down tributaries of the Flinders River. Five members of the Jenkinson family were drowned when their home was swept away by the waters of Betts Creek. The survivors, two sons and two daughters, were saved by John, aged 22, who knocked sheets of iron off the roof, giving the others access to it. The building was carried onto trees to which the young people clung until the flood receded.

The Duncans of Rosevale may well have shared the fate of the Jenkinson family if they had not taken the advice of an old Aborigine and spent the night on higher ground. Next morning their home was gone. At Hughenden the flood swept through the streets at record heights, drowning a young girl on the outskirts of the town when she and her parents tried to reach a neighbour's property.

On the night of Wednesday 27 December, rainfall of over 20 inches (approximately 500 millimetres) was recorded in the Clermont and Capella area. Properties were inundated as creeks rose in record flood. A settler on Theresa Creek perished with his family. This creek, which drained most of the rain-affected areas, spread to seven miles (11 kilometres wide) on its way to join the Nogoa River. At Peak Vale, a station situated near the foot of the Drummond Range, a tributary of Theresa Creek swept through the property in the early morning of the

North Hughenden flood, 2 January 1917. Photo: Courtesy of Stockmans' Hall of Fame

28th. As the floodwater rose in the homestead, Mr W.R. Tindale, the manager of Peak Vale, together with his wife, six children and Vincent Appleton, a visitor, retreated to the top floor. From that vantage point they watched as one after another the station outbuildings were carried away in the torrent. Helpless, they saw the men's huts swept away, drowning an employee by the name of Simpson. Finally the family were forced to build rafts, and took refuge on them until the water receded.

At the Glen, a selection about 20 kilometres from Clermont, Miss Lily Anderson had a narrow escape. She was warned to go to high ground by an Aborigine, the only other person on the place, but she disregarded the advice and was in the house when it was swept from its stumps. She survived by clinging to a door for some 13 hours.

It was Clermont itself, though, that bore the brunt of the flood. In one of the greatest disasters in our history, over 60 residents lost their lives. Part of the town was then built in a bow of Sandy Creek, which ran around the outskirts of the town; a lot of the streets were low lying and some buildings were on the edge of a lagoon that was probably once part of the creek's straighter course. The flood of 1870 had caused both damage and fatalities in the low area between the lagoon and the creek. Wolfang Creek joined Sandy Creek just above the bow where Sandy Creek turned northwards around the town. Wolfang Station had recorded 24 inches (580 millimetres) in 14 hours on the night of the 27th. At daylight on the 28th, Sandy Creek was seen to be in flood, but had not then broken its banks.

The Clermont police warned people living in the low areas, but apparently few took notice of this warning until it was too late. A short time later, huge flood crests in Sandy and Wolfang creeks met and swept through the town to the lagoon and beyond. A man standing on a verandah on the high side of the lagoon saw the huge flood wave and cried out that the sea had broken through to Clermont. To many it must have seemed like this was true. The floodwater rose at the rate of three metres an hour, the main street was inundated, buildings were swept away and many people, trapped by the rapidity of the rise, were drowned.

Miss Rose Harris and her father saved the lives of five men by throwing ropes to them from the top storey of their saddle shop as they were being swept down the street to certain death. A number of residents climbed to the ceilings of business houses, crouching there in terror as the buildings shuddered and swayed in the torrent below. Many took refuge on the top floor of hotels. One enterprising horse had similar ideas; it made its way up the stairs of the Grand Hotel and saw the flood out from the top storey. Getting it back to ground level after the flood passed posed a problem, however, until he was finally backed down the stairs.

Few bushmen swam for pleasure. Apart from bathing, outback waterways held little attraction for stockmen. There is always the exception to the rule, of course, and one tragic instance of this involved twin brothers, both stockmen, who lost their lives while swimming in the Wallam River near Bollon in south-west Queensland. One lad got into difficulties and his brother went to his assistance, resulting in both of them drowning.

The number of bushmen who could not swim has always surprised me, although the ability to swim would not have saved men whose horses caused their death. The list of drowning fatalities that follows is far from complete; however, it gives details of typical outback tragedies.

In 1943 Eric Houghton, a young stockman, drowned while at work crossing cattle at the Georgina River at Camooweal. Vic Stanfield, whom I knew quite well before he became a boss drover, also died in similar circumstances. He was a good type of chap, who, I believe, could swim. When he was a drover in charge of a mob of fat cattle en route to Butru, he was drowned in the Burke River at Picnic Point, just above Boulia. It was not known precisely what happened, but Vic's horse may have got into difficulties crossing the waterhole. When horses panic in water, they behave much like a drowning man and will strike the water, and any object they see, in an attempt to get a foothold. A stockman with Vic saw Vic's riderless horse leave the water and he galloped to the drover's camp, where he told Eugene Costin what had happened. Costin mounted a horse and galloped to the spot where Stanfield had disappeared. There he aided the police in recovering the drover's body.

Most of the inland rivers have claimed victims at one time or another. A young Aboriginal stockman was drowned in the Diamantina when he swam his horse over the river to get some horses that had strayed. A young chap named Fuller, a cousin of the well-known Sam Fuller, was drowned at Abbieglasse in the Wallam. He had ridden into the river after plant horses. The Wallam claimed another victim when a chap known only as 'Buckjump Charlie' drowned near Bollon while swimming his horse over to his camp late one evening. It is believed his horse struck him when it got into difficulties, a common cause of many deaths by drowning.

Linked with outback drownings are the many stories of courageous rescues and rescue attempts. William 'Jack' Oates, aged 35, was a boss drover and a member of a well-known Jundah family. Early in 1956 he was offered a mob of cattle from Bulloo Downs to Broken Hill. When Oates arrived at the station, the mob was not ready, so the drover met the stockcamp on 12 February at Onibootra waterhole. As the drover's plant arrived at the stockcamp, cattle on the opposite side of the hole were disturbed. The Bulloo head stockman shouted to his men to mount up and get the cattle before they got into the thick lignum. Being already mounted, Oates volunteered to help and the party rode down along the waterhole to where it narrowed. It was urgent that the crossing be made quickly, so all the men went into the water fully clothed and with boots and leggings.

The swim was a considerable distance, and halfway over, the horse Oates was riding got into trouble. The drover left his horse as it began striking and plunging, and shortly after, the others saw him disappear. Although fully dressed himself, 17-year-old Bob Findlay left his horse and went to assist Oates. Diving down, he brought the unconscious drover to the surface and started to swim with him to the bank. It was a herculean task and Findlay, although exhausted, refused to let Oates go. The head stockman left his horse to help, but in the changeover Oates slipped away. Findlay came very close to drowning himself, only just managing to reach the bank.

The drover's body was found three days later, caught in the roots of a coolabah tree downstream from where he was lost. The body was removed, placed on a sandhill and covered with bushes to keep dingoes away. One of the stockmen rode into Bulloo Downs Station with the tragic news and the police at Thargomindah were notified. Due to flooded roads, however, the Queensland police could not get to Bulloo, so the New South Wales police at Tibooburra were notified and finally arrived at Onibootra waterhole three days after the body was recovered.

Jack Oates was finally laid to rest on the sandhill. He was buried in his swag and with his boots on. The Royal Humane Society of Australia awarded Bob Findlay its certificate for bravery. Bob now lives at Thargomindah and for some years has been the town's common ranger.

The rivers running into the Gulf of Carpentaria can be death traps in flood, with the fall of these streams far greater than that of inland rivers. Heavy rain on the watersheds of these streams send floodwaters roaring down to the Gulf coast. In 1937 the rainfall was unusually heavy and the Leichhardt, Flinders and other rivers all rose in full flood. In a camp on the bottom end of Clonagh Station, north of Cloncurry, a fencer's wife and two children found themselves trapped by the rising waters of the Corella River. The party phone lines were down and communications were almost non-existent, but word of their plight was received at nearby Cubberoo Station.

Jimmy 'Ringer' Edwards was breaking in horses at Cubberoo and immediately went to the rescue of the stranded family. To bring the fencer's wife and children across the flood, Edwards constructed a boat by upturning a table on a tarpaulin and securing the flaps of the tarp up and over the table. Placing the family in the makeshift boat, Jimmy Edwards towed and pushed the crude but life-saving craft across the flood to safety. It was a fine example of chivalry, guts and bush ingenuity.

At approximately the same time further over to the east, two men attempted to swim their horses across the flooded Flinders River at Black Sam's crossing, just below the town of Richmond. Ted Malone and his mate, another Jimmy Edwards, may have taken the swim rather casually for both were fully dressed when they put their horses into the flood. As in many other cases, the horse ridden by Edwards panicked and began to plunge and strike. Jimmy Edwards disappeared—whether he was struck by the horse is not known, but, being fully clad, he had little chance in a river like the Flinders.

There is a rather tragic footnote to this story. News reached Cloncurry, where the drowned man's family lived, that a Jimmy Edwards had been drowned, but no one knew which one. That is until a few days later when 'Ringer' Edwards rode into the town. One of the children of the drowned man saw Edwards and ran inside crying out that it must have been his dad who had drowned, as he had just seen the other Jimmy Edwards.

All these work-related fatalities occurred when men were swimming horses while mounted. Stockmen have good reason for preferring this method to holding onto their mount's tail and being towed across the creek or river. When stock are being swum over water, they will sometimes start to ring, and stock caught in the middle of the milling mob will inevitably drown. If a man is holding onto the tail of a horse, his eyes will be at water level and he cannot see what is happening, nor would he be able to do anything to rectify the situation if he could.

That is not the only disadvantage to this method. When the far side is reached, the horse has to be caught and can end up amongst the cattle. Not only that, this is a very risky way to cross for anyone who cannot swim, as the tail has to be released before the horse reaches the far bank; not to do so is to risk being kicked. This is exactly how young Colin Cosgrove lost his life. Early in 1957 Colin was working for a drover and on 17 February they began to swim the mob over the Gwydir River. Although he could not swim, Colin elected to hang onto his horse's tail and be towed across. Tragically he held on for too long and was kicked as the horse left the water; Colin slipped back into deep water, unconscious, and was drowned.

Billy Cragg lost his life at a channel crossing on the Stonehenge road. Heavy rain on the headwaters of the channel had sent it roaring down along the Thomson River. Cragg had been horsetailing with a drover's plant that had finished a trip and was returning to Stonehenge. With him were two men, the cook and a young stockman. When they got to the channel, the current was strong and immediately below the crossing the floodwater had gouged out a deep hole in the creek bed that was now a maelstrom of turbulent water. Despite the obvious risk, the three decided to attempt the crossing. The cook, who was driving a horse-drawn wagonette, put the horses into the water, with Cragg riding on the downstream side to keep the team straight. Halfway over the crossing, floodwaters swept the wagonette, horses, and Cragg and his horse into the seething water below. The cook and Billy Cragg's horse managed to escape, but Cragg was drowned, as were the wagonette horses. Billy Cragg's body was later recovered.

Whether at work or pleasure, it is unwise to underestimate the dangers of flooded streams. Billy Ward, a mate of mine, lost his life when he jumped out of a boat that was taking people over the flooded Leichhardt. He intended to beat the boat to the other side of the river. Whether he got a cramp or hit his head is not known, but Billy never made it.

Being reared in North Queensland, I grew up able to swim reasonably well. However, my elder brother, Keith, was a far stronger swimmer. While he was still a teenager he saved a chap named Les Millard from drowning in Owen's Creek. Millard had attempted to cross the creek with

Rowley Wall & Company's mail car in trouble at the flooded Thomson River at Longreach in 1923. Photo: Courtesy of Stockmans' Hall of Fame

Horse-drawn wagonette crossing the flooded Darr River in 1950. Photo: J. Kelly

a two-in-hand buckboard; the current swept horses, vehicle and driver downstream. Keith, seeing Millard's plight, went in and brought him out.

Early in 1969 two large groups from Rutland Plains Station and Mitchell River Mission on the Gulf of Carpentaria met at the mouth of Topsy Creek for a day's fishing. The group included the manager of Rutland Plains, Richard Kriedeman, his wife Marion, daughter Margaret and son David. Kerry Kendall, a stockman, and Norm Smith, the station's camp cook, also went along to wet a line. Arthur White, the overseer of Mitchell River Mission, was there with his family, together with a number of Aborigines from both the station and the mission. Topsy Creek was on the boundary of the two properties, and the combined party settled down to fish after being ferried over to the Rutland Plains side of the tidal creek by Arthur White. Arthur had an aluminium dinghy powered by a small outboard motor, and it took a number of trips to complete the crossing.

The mouth of Topsy Creek, where the ill-fated fishing party met in early 1969. Photo: Kerry Kendall

Apart from being a favourite fishing spot, the mouth of Topsy Creek was also known to be the haunt of saltwater crocs and sharks, but that did not bother the group, at least not then.

The day passed pleasantly enough, the whites fishing for barramundi with rod and reel, while the Aborigines employed their traditional method using fish spears. As the afternoon shadows lengthened, the tide began to ebb and it was decided to ferry the party back to the road side of the creek. On the second last trip the tide was running strongly and the water became very rough. In the boat were Richard Kriedeman, nursing four year old Margaret, Kerry Kendall, with David, aged two, on his lap, Norm Smith and two Aborigines, with White at the motor. When the dinghy was about a third of the way across the creek, disaster struck. The boat capsized, throwing the occupants into the water. Kriedeman and Kendall held onto the children and placed both on the bottom of the overturned boat. Both men were fully dressed and wearing sandshoes, and handicapped as they were—supporting the youngsters—they found it impossible to take off their shoes. The men realised that there was a danger of the tide taking the boat out to sea, and the decision was made to swim back to the bank they had left.

Swimming with one arm and supporting a child in the other, Kriedeman and Kendall set out for the bank, with Norm Smith swimming between them in case they needed help. It was touch and go, but they finally reached safety, both close to exhaustion. There would certainly have been a tragic end to the day's fishing had not every adult in the dinghy been a reasonably good swimmer. The rescue of the two small children was a commendable act of bravery on the part of both men. Kerry Kendall is a very modest chap who says he just did what had to be done.

Another example of selfless courage was demonstrated when Gordon Davidson, a stockman on Mirrambeena Station, north-east of Charters Towers, developed appendicitis. It was early in 1965 and heavy rain had been falling for some time. Despite the weather conditions, Alec Corbett decided to get his mate Gordon to Dotswood Station, where it would be possible to get medical help. However, Keelbottom Creek, a tributary of the Burdekin, was in full flood and would have to be crossed, as Dotswood was 24 kilometres away on the opposite bank. Undaunted, Alec fuelled up a tractor, the only vehicle he thought might be able to negotiate the boggy conditions. He made Gordon comfortable and set off, hoping to attract attention when he reached the creek bank opposite Dotswood.

The dice seemed to be loaded against the attempt, for they had not gone far when the tractor became bogged to the axles. Alec was not a man who gave up easily, though. Leaving his mate with the tractor, he walked back to Mirrambeena, caught and saddled two horses and hastened back to the sick man. He helped Gordon to mount the spare horse and they set off again towards Dotswood. Gordon was by this time very sick indeed and Alec had to support him in the saddle. Eventually the pair reached a spot on the creek bank opposite Dotswood and Alec managed to alert the station of the situation.

Alec knew it would not be possible to swim the horses over the flooded creek, as he would not be able to support the sick man once the horses were in the water. While he considered his options, the manager of Dotswood got a young chap who was a strong swimmer to cross over to give assistance. Realising that Gordon needed urgent medical attention, Alec took two stirrup leathers off his saddle, and buckling them together, he slipped them on like a bandolier. He put one of the patient's arms through the strap, then entered the water, swimming with one arm and supporting Gordon with the other. Bernie Mossman, the chap who had swum over to help, started swimming with Alec, but the current took him well downstream while Alec swam almost straight across.

The sick man was put to bed at Dotswood and the flying doctor contacted. Thanks to the courage and determination of Alec Corbett, Gordon Davidson made a full recovery.

It is always a traumatic experience for families when isolated by floodwaters. Typical of the parlous situation many families have faced is the one Lucky Forrester found himself in during mid-August 1954 while managing Maramarai Station. Heavy rain fell on the headwaters and tributaries of the Condamine River and Tchanning Creek, and banked up by floodwaters downstream, surrounded the homestead that was situated on a sandhill. This situation would not normally cause concern, but Lucky's wife Eileen, who was eight months pregnant, and his two-year-old daughter Irene were alone with him on the place.

It was impossible for a plane to land on the flooded property and the only phone contact the family had was with a neighbour. As the time for Eileen's confinement grew closer and the floodwater showed no signs of receding, Lucky realised he would have to get the family out on horseback, which involved wading and swimming for over a kilometre. That should have been straightforward enough, although risky, but therein lay a problem. Lucky had only two horses in hand: one was a very poor swimmer—the type that kept plunging down to feel for the bottom—and the other one, although a good swimmer, was prone to buck.

Lucky overcame the problem by leading the touchy horse into the floodwater before helping his wife into the saddle. Once in the water, the horse forgot about playing up. Lucky took his daughter on the poor swimmer, and the couple set out to cross the flooded claypans and channels. Every time Lucky felt his mount start to dive for the bottom, he told his little girl to take a deep breath. Apparently his daughter thought it was all quite good fun The family finally reached dry land none the worse for the ordeal and Mrs Forrester was taken to hospital in Miles, where shortly afterwards the couple's son David was born.

I doubt if there is a better example of the combined beauty and menace found in the Australian bush than the Burdekin River. Its tributaries drain a huge area that is subject to heavy seasonal rain. During the dry periods of the year, it is a tranquil and beautiful stream, its crystal clear waters gliding gently past sand shoals and rocky outcrops. The first white men to encounter the Burdekin, Ludwig Leichhardt and his party—who were on their way to Port Essington—travelled north up the river, feasting on the fruit from the native plum trees as they went. In the wet, however, the great river changes character. Huge volumes of floodwaters from the Belyando and its northern tributaries roar down, turning the Burdekin into an immense and turbulent torrent.

The Burdekin has been responsible for many deaths since white settlement. In his book *North Queensland Cavalcade*, Fred Bagnell lists the names of some 70 people who have drowned in the river or its tributaries. Many of the victims, children among them, lost their lives due to misadventure while swimming, or at outings and picnics. Others were drowned during floods. Fate can be cruel, as we all know, and it proved to be so in the case of Laurence Bryant, a stockman who lost his life when crossing the Burdekin in 1947. Laurence's grandfather, Harry Bryant, a teamster, had drowned in the Burdekin in almost the same spot, not far from Burdekin Downs Station, in 1899. One of the victims claimed by the Broughton River, which joins the Burdekin below Sellheim, was the head stockman on Fanning Downs, Jack Williams, who drowned in 1964 while trying to remove cattle from the river.

Bushman Mick Perks at the monument erected on the bank of the Burdekin in honour of Ludwig Leichhardt and his party. Photo: Kerry Kendall

Every wet season the Burdekin River isolated North Queensland, cutting both road and rail between Home Hill and Ayr. The low level rail bridge built in 1913 was totally ineffective. This structure, called the Inkerman Bridge, was 732 metres long and just three metres above water level; it rose to the river bank at a 1 in 33 gradient. In 1917, in 1923 and again in 1940 this bridge was destroyed by raging floods. During these periods rail passengers were ferried over the swollen river by a small boat with an outboard motor.

Twice I made the hazardous boat trip over the flooded Burdekin, which stretched for some 700 metres from bank to bank. The first time I was only three years old, but the memory is still quite vivid. In 1926 my father went north to inspect a property he was thinking of buying. He took his family with him, and at Home Hill the Burdekin was found to be in full flood. When our turn came, we stepped gingerly into the boat and headed for the northern side of the river. I wasn't too worried until I looked at my mother; she was as pale as a ghost and obviously terrified. Fear can be contagious and when we disembarked I found that my pants were wet. I'm afraid floodwater was not to blame.

The remains of the Burdekin bridge after one of the many floods that cut the line to the North. Photo: North Queensland Register

My second ferry ride over the flooded Burdekin, in the mid-1950s, was far less stressful. I had been on holidays in Brisbane and caught the Cairns Mail, planning to head west from Townsville on the train to Mount Isa. A mate of mine, Tidly Treffett, had also been holidaying in the big smoke and I was pleased to meet him at Roma Street, also heading north. Tidly was a bit of a larrikin and great company, which resulted in a thoroughly enjoyable journey north. At Bororen we indulged ourselves in the meat pies that had made the little town famous. They were, Tidly pronounced, 'The best bloody pies ever made.' When the train stopped at Rockhampton the pair of us made for the refreshment room and ordered beers; we had both sampled the local brew before and knew its reputation for being virtually undrinkable at times. We looked at one another ruefully and agreed there seemed little improvement; we ordered another round nevertheless.

Flood damage to the bridge over the Burdekin, March 1945. Taken shortly after the train disaster that took two lives. Photo: *North Queensland Register*

At Home Hill we discovered the old Burdekin problem had reared its ugly head again. A disembodied voice advised us to leave the train with all luggage and line up beside the tracks to wait for transport by boat over the Burdekin. Tidly and I grabbed our swags from the luggage compartment and climbed down. The sight that met our eyes was disconcerting. We had been in the last carriage and ahead of us now was a queue that stretched for hundreds of metres.

Tidly, however, was not a man to accept inconvenience if he could do something about it. Shouldering his swag, he turned to me and said, 'Let's get going.' He then marched along the line of passengers, with me following. Tidly completely ignored the glares of the long-suffering travellers, and we got to the bank of the Burdekin just as the boat pulled in. Without hesitation, my mate heaved his swag into the little craft and followed it. I joined him, rather expecting to be thrown out again, but neither the train guard nor the boatman said a word. After a few other passengers had climbed aboard, the boat set out for the Ayr side of the Burdekin. As the little boat fought its way across the turbulent floodwaters, I thought about my first crossing. As then, our freeboard was no more than 10 centimetres. My mate was quite unconcerned, but I pulled my boots off just in case.

Shortly after, we were seated in a pub in Ayr with a cold beer in front of us. 'People are like sheep,' Tidly said sagely. 'They'll jump through any hoop, as long as some clown in authority tells them to do it.' I believed his judgement of our fellow passengers to be a trifle harsh but nodded agreement. At the same time I thought to myself that if the world was full of hard cases like Tidly, life could become rather interesting, if at times chaotic.

During the wet season of 1945 the Burdekin claimed two victims. Shortly before 4 a.m. on 8 March a mixed train on its way south pulled into the Ayr railway station. The train consisted mainly of empty wagons but had six wagons full of bullocks, totalling about 100 head. There was also a carriage for passengers and, of course, a guard's van, manned by railway guard Jim Ford. There were already three passengers aboard when the train pulled into Ayr. Cecil Felstead had been on the train since Cairns and was travelling to Mackay. Two brothers, Jack and Leslie Swensen, had also come from further north.

Three other passengers joined the train at Ayr to travel to Keebah siding, south of Home Hill. They were George Pemble, aged 16, Neil

A train crosses the old bridge over the Burdekin—the floodwater is just below the track in the middle of the bridge. Photo: Courtesy of Stockmans' Hall of Fame

Christensen, in his mid-20s and Norman Linton, aged 22. Before leaving Ayr, Bill Thomson, the driver of the train, and the guard were advised that the Burdekin was in flood and the water was about one metre under the Inkerman Bridge. The train proceeded south and started across the bridge. At that time there was still no water on the line, but there was debris deposited by earlier rises in the river. Halfway over the bridge, a piece of this debris ruptured the Westinghouse brake lines between the engine and the tender. This slammed on the brakes of the whole train, bringing it to a grinding stop. It was a situation fraught with danger, for the river had begun to rise. Bill Thomson and his fireman, Errol Gregory, uncoupled the engine and tender and set out to the Home Hill side of the river to effect repairs. By the time they reached the southern bank, water was beginning to cover the line in the middle of the bridge. The rest of the train, stranded on the low middle section, was now in real danger of being swept away by the rising floodwaters.

Realising the danger, Christensen and some other passengers, including the Swensens, decided to try and walk to the Home Hill side. Froth and debris were now being swept down with the flood crest, forcing them to crawl along on the trucks. On arriving at the end of the train, they saw that walking out was impossible due to the current, and returned to where Jim Ford was calling for help to release the cattle. Christensen started opening the doors of the front cattle truck when the front part of the train was swept from the bridge. He turned to see the two brothers flung into the water. The whole train then began to go over and Jim Ford and the rest of the passengers were hurled into the turbulent wall of water that was sweeping down the Burdekin.

The doors on three cattle trucks had been opened before the train was swept off the bridge. Most of the men in the water were able to grab onto the tails of bullocks, an action that saved their lives. Amid the confusion and debris, Christensen finally managed to get hold of the tail of a bullock that was heading downstream. After being towed along for some distance, the beast became stuck in the fork of a huge log that was being borne along by the torrent. Christensen decided to abandon the tail in favour of the log. Some time later Ford, Linton and Felstead, who came by on bullocks' tails, joined him on the tree trunk. At one time during their journey on the log they had to fight off bullocks that were trying to share their haven.

The huge log finally became fouled in trees some eight kilometres below the bridge. A rescue boat with Sergeant Linnane in charge picked them up from there. Pemble was also rescued, by a boat manned by Constable Lewis and two volunteers. The two Swensen brothers, who went into the river with the front part of the train, were drowned. Had it not been for the cattle, the death toll would probably have been a lot higher.

The Burdekin continued to cut links to the north until 1957, when a new high level bridge was finally constructed and the turbulent waters of the Burdekin were tamed at last.

Late in November 1951 Jack O'Loughlin, a 25-year-old stockman, lost his life in tragic and unusual circumstances. He and his mate Laurie Hansen had worked on a number of cattle stations in North Queensland, and they spent the last part of the 1951 stock season on Van Rook Station. I knew both of them quite well, as they came from the same area as I did, west of Mackay. In fact, Laurie and I were connected by a terrible accident that occurred when Laurie's father was commissioned by my father to transport lumber to build a house on his recently taken up selection. As a result of an accident with the team, Laurie's father lost half of one foot and my father lost all the timber for the house.

After the cattle work finished on Van Rook, Jack and Laurie were

Laurie Hansen, left, taken with the author in February 1999 at Finch Hatton, Qld. Photo: Kerry Kendall

employed at the station. On Monday 26 November Jack O'Loughlin was working on a saw bench with an Aboriginal offsider. Laurie, with another Aborigine, was some distance away collecting firewood in a dray. At 11 a.m. Jack started to cut a twisted and forked log when the circular saw jammed and a large piece of timber flew back, striking him in the face. He received serious facial injuries and was unconscious for some time. When he did finally recover consciousness, he seemed dazed and lacked coordination. The Cairns Aerial Ambulance was called and the plane, a Dragon Rapide, was dispatched at 1.40 p.m. with Captain Neville Hicks at the controls. Ambulance bearer Keith Howarth accompanied the pilot.

The plane landed at Van Rook, 254 miles (406 kilometres) west of Cairns, O'Loughlin's injuries were dressed, and he was placed on board the aircraft. As the pair had decided to return home for Christmas, Laurie Hansen asked if he could travel to Cairns as well. Captain Hicks had no objection and the plane took off at 5 p.m. with the four men on board.

North Queensland was very dry at the time and smoke from bushfires and low cloud made navigation difficult right from the start. The pilot got his bearings from Wrotham Park Station, and advised Cairns that his ETA was 7.25 p.m. However, as the aircraft got closer to its destination, visibility became worse until finally the terrain became completely blanketed with smoke and cloud. Landing at Cairns under those conditions, Captain Hicks felt, was impossible; the closeness of the sea and the high mountains behind the town gave little room for error. The time was now half past seven and the pilot had no course of action other than to circle around in the hope of the visibility improving.

At that point both the pilot and ambulance bearer were in the cockpit, O'Loughlin was lying on a stretcher with a strap over him and Hansen was sitting on a lower seat. Fuel was getting low and Hansen's recollections are that radio contact had been tried unsuccessfully for some time. With the fuel almost exhausted, Captain Hicks decided to ditch the plane in the sea. Keith Howarth came back and told Laurie and Jack what the situation was, then showed them how to release the strap on the stretcher and open the escape hatch above it.

As he didn't know how close he was to the ranges, Captain Hicks decided it was better to err on the side of caution, and put the aircraft into the water some three kilometres from land. There can be no doubt that Captain Hicks' decision was correct, nor any doubt that the ditching was skilfully handled. Despite reports to the contrary, however, Laurie Hansen is positive the plane sank almost at once. By the time he had released his seatbelt, water was rushing in from the plane's ruptured side, and he had to wait for the water pressure to stabilise before getting out. He remembers having to swim upwards for at least two strokes to reach the surface. As he swam towards the other three, he bumped into a floating seat cushion, which was given to Jack O'Loughlin when he joined the others. All four of the men on board were shaken and slightly hurt in the ditching, and the already seriously injured O'Loughlin was now in a bad way, dazed, disoriented and fighting efforts to help him.

It was now dark and the men were not sure how far out to sea they were, nor in which direction the coast lay. Laurie still remembers the struggle he had pulling off his boots and getting out of his jodhpurs. He almost drowned in the effort. The three who were relatively fit had to support O'Loughlin, who was a poor swimmer at the best of times; now badly injured, he could do little to help himself. The visibility at water level was not much better than it had been in the air. All that could be seen on the horizon was a dim smudge, until Laurie, a good bushman, saw the evening star above the haze. Some time later the lights of cars could be seen on the coast road. The party set off swimming towards the coast, with Jack O'Loughlin being supported on the cushion. All three of them could swim, but the task of controlling the semi-conscious O'Loughlin made progress slow and difficult.

The knowledge that the waters off Cairns were the haunt of sharks made the struggle to reach safety a nightmare. Finally it was decided that Laurie Hansen, who was the strongest swimmer, should go on alone and try and get help. He set out, leaving Jack on the cushion being helped by Hicks and Howarth, who had stripped down to their underpants. After five hours in the water, Laurie heard breakers and shortly afterwards he thankfully crawled up the sand of a beach north of Cairns. Initially he had difficulty in standing, but after a few minutes he set off and came to the Cook Highway. He turned south and continued on in the hope of finding help for his mate and the other two men still in the water. Unknown to Hansen, Captain Hicks and Keith Howarth were now swimming on their own, having lost O'Loughlin some two hours into the swim.

Meanwhile the aircraft had been reported missing, but the authorities had no idea where it might have come down. An RAAF fix put the aircraft near Mareeba, and a call for assistance was answered by many motorists, who lit up the Mareeba aerodrome with their headlights. The Cairns police were notified and Inspector W. Peters decided it might be worthwhile taking a run up the Cook Highway.

At 11 p.m. he set out with two constables and at 2.45 a.m. the police party met Laurie Hansen walking towards Cairns. He told them of the ditching and asked for a boat. As there was none available, the inspector drove on and later picked up Captain Hicks and ambulance bearer Howarth. The three men were taken to Cairns hospital suffering from shock and minor injuries. Next morning an aerial search was organised to try and locate Jack O'Loughlin's body. Unfortunately this was unsuccessful—his body was never found.

Past Inverway

Oh! the West seemed full of promise
And the bush asked little from us,
When we rode the track that led us
Out to where our future lay.
And we left but few hearts grieving
At the prospect of our leaving,
Like the wild geese heading westward,
Further out past Inverway.

With the plant shod up we started
On our pilgrimage, light hearted,
With the hobble chains a-jingle
And the loaded packs a-sway.
But we'd little more to guide us
Than the faith that rode beside us,
When at first we travelled westward
Further out past Inverway.

Then the wattle scent was spreading
And the boughs their blossoms shedding
Made a golden fairy carpet
Where the dappled shadows lay.
Then the wet had not long ended
And the grass like wheat extended
From the old road heading westward,
Further out past Inverway.

When we camped the evening found us
With the virgin bush around us,
While the horses grazed in hobbles
lest they wander off and stray.
Down the flat their bells were ringing
As the Southern Cross was swinging
Up above the darkened timber,
Further out past Inverway.

As the night wind softly blowing
Set the back-log embers glowing,
We yarned of future triumphs
Where the last frontier lay.
We awoke each dew-drenched dawning
To the music of the morning,
As the bush birds gave us welcome
Further out past Inverway.

Then we had no qualms not knowing
What awaited us, when going
Out to where the wild geese gathered
And the brolgas danced at play,
For the sap of youth was flowing,
And our spirits soared when going
Out to Kimberley, our mecca,
Further out past Inverway.

After Buchanan

Nat Buchanan and the other early overlanders left a legacy of outstanding droving achievement. After their departure others took up the challenge of overcoming the natural hazards and the tyranny of distance that stood between far-flung stations and the markets. They were to prove worthy successors to the men who opened up the country.

To many people in Australia, droving is no more than a rather romantic interlude in our past—a chapter that was romanticised by poets like Ogilvie and Paterson. In truth there was little romance in droving, but it was one of the most important industries in this country. Since early settlement Australia has depended largely on its pastoral wealth. No station could have been established or could have operated without the help of drovers, first of all to stock the runs and later to take the stock to market. Prior to the early 1960s, each year thousands of mobs of cattle and sheep travelled the vast network of stockroutes that crisscrossed this country.

The lead of a mob of Manbulloo store bullocks crossing the Rankine Plain.

No, droving was no romantic interlude. For over 150 years it was one of the mainstays of our nation. During that period everyone who sat down to a meal of chops or steak, or carved a Sunday roast, had a drover to thank for his or her meal. The railways in Australia did not extend into the vast cattle country as they did in America, where they put an end to routes like the Chisholm trail after just 28 years of operation. The Kimberley and Northern Territory stations established by Buchanan, the Duracks, the Farquharsons and others remain as isolated from markets today as they did back before the turn of the century.

In an attempt to open a stockroute from the Kimberley runs to the West Australian goldfields, A.W. Canning, a government surveyor, set out in 1906 from Wiluna and travelled north to Billiluna. Two years later he opened the route that still bears his name. Water was scarce and Canning opened and deepened Aboriginal waterholes to provide stock water. The nomadic Aborigines of the area resented the intrusion of whites into their tribal lands, and in 1910 when the first mob attempted to travel the Canning, they struck. A small mob of about 200 head was started down to Wiluna. With the cattle were drovers Thompson and Shoesmith and one Aboriginal stockman. Late one afternoon when the men were in camp, they were attacked by Aborigines and all three were killed.

Tom Cole (not the author) took a small mob down the torturous track the same year and got through. Later Wickham and McManus followed. The Canning route then fell idle until 1930, when Canning again opened it up to cattle. Men like Dick Rowan and later Wally Dowling took cattle down to Wiluna, using whips, a system of ropes and pulleys harnessed to a camel, to draw water from the wells. Dowling used camels successfully during his trips on the Canning. However, the route was never used to any great extent.

The meatworks at Wyndham, established during World War I, did a little to ease the burden of isolation by providing a limited market closer at hand. Mobs of forward store bullocks (bullocks in good condition) from the East Kimberley region and from the western part of the Territory walked to the works at Wyndham. Vestry's huge meatworks, also built during World War I, was a white elephant, however. Erected at Bullocky's Point near Darwin, it closed down in 1919. Many claimed the company built the works with an eye to securing grazing leases rather than the processing of meat. Whatever the motive, the white ants took over and the stations continued to be

Victoria River Downs bullocks watering at the East Baines River on their way to Wyndham meatworks. Drover John White was in charge. Photo: Ray Hulbert

forced to send their store bullocks down the long and lonely stockroutes to Queensland.

The boss drovers who brought the big store bullocks in were for the most part tough characters. Hard conditions breed hard men; the stockroutes of the North-West were no place for cream puffs. Boss drovers bore a heavy responsibility, having the welfare of cattle, horses and men on their shoulders. It has been said that there was no one above them to pass the buck to but God. They were an un-Godly lot, however, who spoke to God but seldom and then never in a manner likely to engender a sympathetic response from their maker.

Droving trips of 1600 kilometres were common during the period between the turn of the century and the early 1960s. Drovers took store bullocks from the East Kimberley stations to the trucks at Dajarra or to fattening properties in Queensland. Bullocks from the Northern Territory runs followed the same route, while cattle from stations in the Queensland Gulf often walked the stockroutes down into New South Wales and at times into Victoria.

One would need a complete book to list all the outstanding droving feats of those days; a few typical examples will suffice here. In 1930

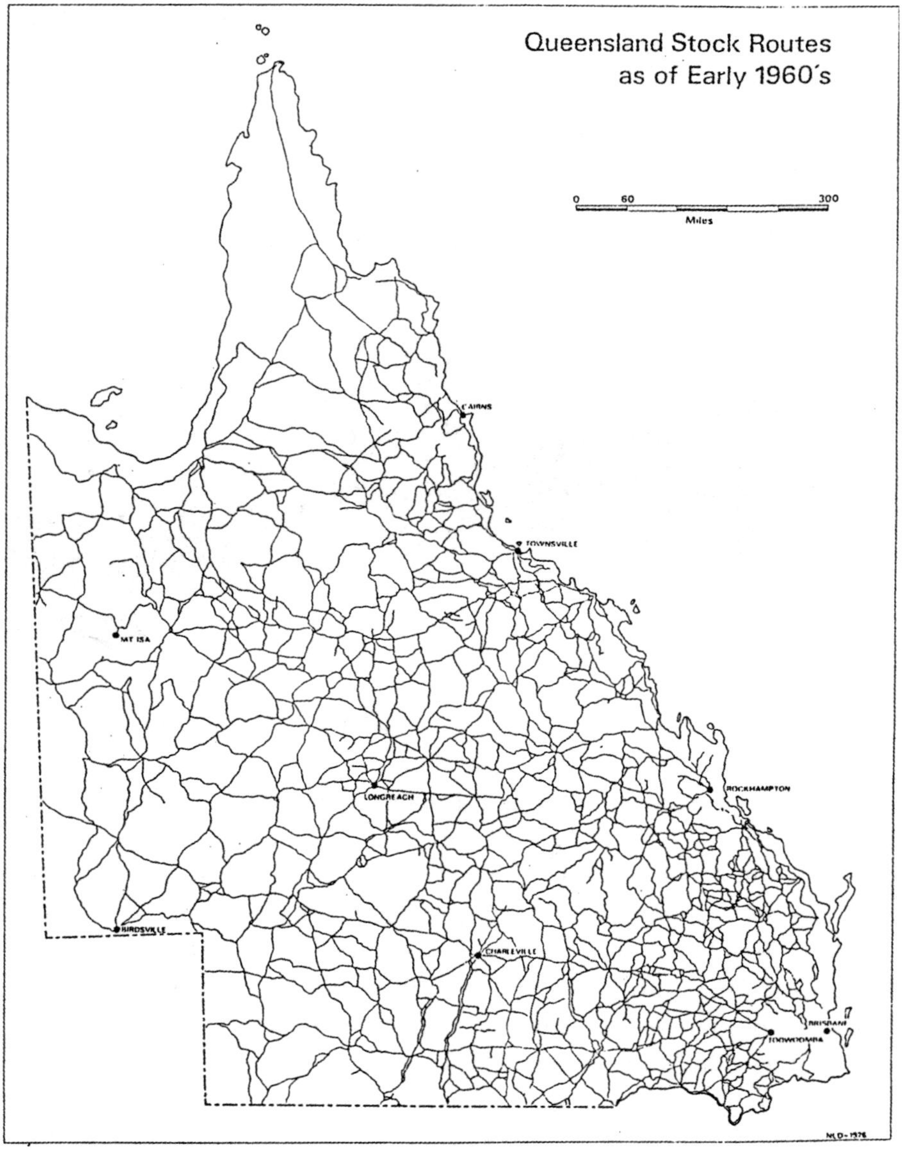

Queensland stockroutes of the early 1960s. (Based on various maps, Queensland Dept of Public Lands, Brisbane)

legendary Kidman drover Jim Laffin drove 1250 bullocks from Alexandria in the Northern Territory to Glengyle Station in the Channel Country of Queensland. After a week's spell he took the top 500 of them to the trucks at Marree in South Australia. Sam Cousins and his sons picked up a mob

The author, right, with 92-year-old ex-Kidman drover Jim Laffin (Snr).
Photo: George Ellis

of bullocks from Wave Hill, Northern Territory in the 1930s. After travelling the stockroutes of the Territory and Queensland for almost 3000 kilometres, the mob was delivered at Clive Station near Marlborough, only a short distance from the Queensland coast. It was reported that some of the mob from Wave Hill had previously walked there from Yeda and other stations on the West Australian coast. If this is correct, some of the cattle delivered at Clive had walked across Australia from west to east.

In the 1930s Bob Iles, later a boss drover himself, worked for Billy Hall. Hall took delivery of 1500 store bullocks from Dalgonally Station in the Queensland Gulf Country; eight months later he delivered the mob at Cubby near Bourke in New South Wales. During a drought year Jack Jackson, a boss drover from Barcaldine, took delivery of a mob of store bullocks from Avon Downs in the Northern Territory. The mob was put on the road for grass, Jackson taking them down the Georgina, then on to Birdsville. With a five-in-hand team of mules, Jackson then crossed into South Australia over the sandhills at Haddon's corner, the only drover ever to do this. The mob was taken on down the Strzelecki Track. Jackson then turned the mob back on advice from the owners, and from Birdsville he travelled the mob down to the border with New South

Group of ex-drovers and ringers at Camooweal, 1997. Left to right: Herb Huemiller, George Booth, Ernie McCarthy, Blue Ellis, Alf Champers, the author, Ian 'Spud' Tait; Front: the late Bob McDonald and the late John Gardner. Photo: the late John Gardner

Wales. Crossing the border, Jackson finally trucked the bullocks away at Walgett after 41 weeks on the road.

In 1954 boss drover Bob Iles took delivery of 1500 head of dry cows from Newcastle Waters Station in the Northern Territory. The mob was travelling for sale. Iles travelled the mob down to Augathella, where the cows were spelled for a month. Iles then picked the mob up again and crossed over into New South Wales, taking the mob to Bourke, then on to Walgett. With the mob still unsold, Iles crossed back into Queensland, then south again. At Brewarrina the mob was at last sold. The travelling time for the trip was 10 months.

The above are just some of the droving trips done in the past by the men who followed in the footsteps of the early overlanders. There are many other stories that could be told: tales of Tom 'One Potato Tom' Starr, of Paddy Conway, called 'Beef Eye' by the Aborigines, of Walter Cowan and Jack Carroll, drovers who took cattle off Rocklands Station for 49 years and 50 years respectively, of that legendary drover of later years, Noel 'Pic' Willetts, the last drover to bring cattle through the notorious Murranji track.

Typical of the top men who worked for boss drovers is Tom Cusack. A veteran of the notorious Birdsville, Strzelecki and Murranji tracks, Tom knew every stockroute in the North-West like the back of his hand. He worked for a number of old-time drovers and in 1962 he was droving with Paddy Fogarty. After delivering a mob at Clifton Hills Station in South Australia, Fogarty was offered two mobs off Billiluna Station, just south of Hall's Creek in Western Australia. Paddy was advised to take his plant to Marree and go by train to Alice Springs. At this time he was using a truck and trailer to cart his droving gear. In due course, men, fresh horses and vehicles arrived in the Alice. Fogarty's droving team consisted of his father, Lloyd Snr, and his sons Lloyd, Stan and Jack, with Tom making up the normal crew of five men and the boss.

The plant horses were trucked up the Tanami track to Mount Doreen Station, the destination of the first mob, then driven over the West Australian–Northern Territory border to Billiluna. When Paddy and the others arrived with the plant, the mob of 1860 store bullocks was not yet fully mustered. The drovers agreed to hold the mob in hand as the muster progressed. It was the first time a large mob would ever attempt to travel down the Tanami track. The year before a small mob of 400 had travelled down as a test run, but it was the mob from Billiluna that would really open the route.

Things did not go well for the drovers during the muster. First young Jack developed appendicitis and was taken to Balgo Mission, and from there by the flying doctor to Derby Hospital. Shortly afterwards Stan broke his arm when his horse fell while mustering around Lake Gregory. Paddy was two men short and the trip had not even started. When the mob was ready, however, the manager of Billiluna lent the drover two Aboriginal ringers for the trip.

They took delivery of the bullocks and started off, facing a dry stage of nearly 130 kilometres. Now, a dry stage of that magnitude can be a problem with broken-in road bullocks; to negotiate it with fresh cattle is a formidable task that calls for expert cattle work. Against the odds the mob was taken through safely, the truck delivering water for the horses at each camp. After a week on the road the mob started rushing (the Australian term for stampede), and continued to rush for up to four times a night during the whole trip.

As Paddy and Tom were the only members of the team with experience with rushing bullocks, they got little rest at night, but were able to

Tommy Cusack at the Camooweal reunion, 1998. Photo: Spud Tait

snatch a bit of sleep on dinner camp. At Lake Alexandria (a dry lake) they found themselves dealing with a very bad rush, with the bullocks almost going over the camp. Next morning there were bullock tracks hurdling Tom's swag.

One of Tom's jobs was to track around wide of the ground where the mob had been the night before. If tracks showed bullocks had got away, he tracked them and brought them back. On one occasion he was away for three days getting bullocks that had cleared out.

There were many dry stages to cross and because of slow water supply the drovers were forced to use the pump they carried to augment the flow from bores. But after dust storms, dry stages and constant rushes, the mob was finally delivered at Mount Doreen. Paddy Fogarty was sometimes known as 'Piebald Paddy' because of his liking for coloured horses, but he was no mug with galloping bullocks and he had a top man with him in Tom. The Tanami track was open.

After a couple of days' spell the drovers headed back to Billiluna to pick up the second mob. En route they enjoyed the hospitality of Father McGuire and the nuns at the mission. Again the mob numbered 1860 store bullocks. Paddy's two sons, now both fully recovered, joined the drovers. This time the mob was destined for Mount Riddock Station, north-east of Alice Springs, a trip of over 1200 kilometres. It was far from the longest droving trip, but the nature of the route made it an epic. The same 130 kilometre dry stage had to be faced, and again the bullocks rushed almost every night and there were problems with the water supply.

After counting the mob at Chilla Wells, some of the bullocks strayed into the timber. As he rode over to turn them back, Tom noticed what looked like a white tarpaulin some distance away. Closer inspection revealed the tarp was over a Volkswagen, and on the back seat was a dead man. A hose from the exhaust into the car appeared to be the cause of death. In due course the police were notified and Tom went back with them to show them the vehicle and body. Later Tom learnt that the body in the car was that of an English journalist, who had apparently chosen to drive out into the desert to end it all.

At Amburla the drovers found short green feed and herbage. If cattle have been on dry feed for a long time, grazing on this type of feed will cause them to bloat; that is, there will be a large build up of gas in their stomachs. The condition, if not treated, is usually fatal. The old bush remedy is simple—a pocket knife blade is driven into the paunch at the right place and out whistles the gas; the small wound quickly heals. Fourteen of Paddy's mob went down with the bloat, but Paddy and Tom, being experienced men, put the old method to work and saved all but four.

It was now starting to get late in the season and the temperature often soared above the 120°F (49°C) mark; the ground reading would have been around 160°F (71°C) or 170°F (77°C). Tom recalls seeing 'phantom rain' on more than one occasion. This phenomenon only occurs in extremely hot weather in dry desert country areas: rain can be seen falling from clouds but evaporates before it reaches the ground.

Although still rushing on some nights, the mob had settled down a bit when the drovers turned the bullocks up the Plenty Highway towards Mount Riddock Station, where they were delivered on 27 October.

Both droving trips were regarded as epics and received quite a lot of publicity. Sadly there are only two survivors of those outstanding trips. Jack Fogarty lives in Winton in Western Queensland. He works for the electrical authority there and on weekends is a keen opal gouger. Tom Cusack, his droving days far behind him, now works on Mittibah Station in the Northern Territory. One of his greatest enjoyments in life is meeting his old droving mates at the drovers' reunion held at Camooweal in August each year.

They were tough characters, the old-time drovers, but great Australians who brought the beef to the tables of our city dwellers. There is still some droving done today, but the days are gone when the great mobs stretched down the stockroutes, a day's stage between them, for hundreds of kilometres. It is estimated that in 1953, 150,000 head of cattle went on the road in the North-West. To move that number, over 100 drovers with their men and horses would have been required. I am proud to say that I was one of those drovers. During the first 60 years of this century the stockroutes of Australia were alive with movement; the sound of hoof beats and stock whips, of horse bells and hobbles, was music to a horseman's ears. Droving was a tough job; we ate rough tucker and slept on the ground in thin swags, yet even if I could I would not change a day of my time on the stockroutes.

The Daylight Watch

The daylight watch is a graveyard shift,
From three till the dawn comes stealing,
While a billion stars in the heavens drift
To the planet's steady wheeling.
The cross hangs low in the southern sky
As the last watch slowly passes,
No bullock stirs as my horse goes by
Hooves quiet on the dew-damp grasses.

I ride on watch with a loose-held rein,
My tryst with the darkness keeping
Round the cattle camp on the narrow plain,
Where the big store mob is sleeping.
I ride and sing lest the mob take fright
And rush like a torrent flowing,
To smash forever the calm of night
In the wake of their frantic going.

I watch and wait for the glow of dawn
That will herald the coming morrow,
But night holds sway and the curlews mourn
Like souls in the vale of sorrow.
It's an eerie shift for a man alone
Ere dawn when the night is dying,
A chill wind blows and the gidgees moan
As ghosts of the past come sighing.

Bill Cousins, whose father brought bullocks from Wave Hill, Northern Territory to Clive Station, near Marlborough in Queensland. Photo: Ernie McCarthy

The Lament of a Cow and Calf Drover

Mixed cattle thirteen hundred head, they spread across the plain,
We pause a while to curse our fate then start them up again.
With waterholes at every turn and feed at every stride
The bloated breeders walk so slow you'd think them petrified.
It's little use, we realise, to flog or rave or stamp,
The lead departs, the wings expand, the tail decides to camp.

A thousand miles we brought the plant, it spelled down at the 'fort'
A thousand long and lonely miles for bullocks, so we thought.
We would have welcomed weaner steers, or stags, or even both,
As every ringer here declared upon his crimson oath.
But cows and calves! Our hearts rebel and with one scorching breath
We wish on every cow and calf a fate far worse than death.

The bovine birth rate's on the rise—a packhorse drover's blight,
Each morn we curse the newborn calves, arrivals of the night.
The old night horses that would fight to catch a flying lead
Go round the mob with grudging step to turn the strays that feed.
Eight miles a day they've put us on, eight weary miles a day
Along the green and watered road that passes Inverway.

The billabongs are brimming full, the bush with music rings,
The grass is blowing tall and sweet from here to Helen Springs.
The coolibahs are fresh and green, and bright blue are the skies
And with a lively mob of stores we'd call it paradise.
But cows and calves! We grind our teeth and gibber in our sleep,
A man should give the North away and go a-droving sheep.

Oh! one must be a stoic born to stay sane and succeed
At droving blasted cows and calves that have a bullock lead.
Still I suppose things could be worse, the springs could all go dry—
The bores could all be broken down across the Murranji,
The ringer lads could catch the blight—the nags catch 'walkabout'
The publicans along the road could all forget to shout.

So we will bear our bovine cross, although we cannot grin.
And do a spot of penance now for some forgotten sin.
We'll keep the old hides plodding on along the pads and ride
Like demons down the spreading wings to stem the bawling tide.
We'll tear our hair and curse our fate here where the road dust clings
And dream of that delivery date ahead at Helen Springs.

Lake Nash bullocks on the road in the early 1930s. Photo: the late Bob Gordon

Manbulloo bullocks stringing out over the Barkly Tableland, 1953.

DATE	
Oct. 17	returned & camped at O'Reilly's – Gill there –
Oct. 18	Saw Booth at Rocklands East with 1332 – Also Herro Travers on Bitumen – Arrived Isa 2 p.m. –
Oct. 25	Left Isa – Saw Laffin at Rocklands West & Rankine not far out – Simpson at Avon Bore, Sherwin at O'Reilly's – Back to Avon Bore & saw Travers then on & camped below Soudan –
Oct. 26	On & saw Laffin's mob in Quarrantine Reserve – Laffin in Dajarra – Saw Turner near Dip – Onto "the Dangie" – Saw Phil Hanlon – Camped Walgra –
Oct. 27	Returned Isa via Moonah Crk. Bores – Plenty water – Saw J. White

DATE	
Oct. 27	at 4 Mile & Bill Sharpe at 12 Mile – Hollins at Oban Bore –
Nov. 2nd	Left Isa – Camped Arcadia –
Nov. 3rd	Onto Lake Nash – Saw Kerro Jago – up to Laffin then back & saw Turner at "the Dangie" – Camped Rochedale –
Nov. 4th	Onto Isa –
Nov. 6th	Left for Camooweal with McGregor (Bookkeeper) – Saw Britt who met him – Onto Avon No 6 & camped –
Nov. 7th	Saw Sherwin then back to Isa –
Nov. 10th	Left Isa – Through Barclay & saw Standfield at Bucket Hole – Back to Lake Nash Dip & camped –
Nov. 11	Saw P. Pedwell dipping – Laffin about 5 miles further down – Turner at Moonah Crk. Bore – Returned Isa –

Jim Pearson was second in charge to Gilbert Macintosh, Vestry's road boss.
By kind permission of Jim Pearson

Barlow Jackson's plant taking Avon Downs cows across the flooded Alice River, Queensland in 1950. The drover in charge was Claude Burns (in overcoat at edge of river). Photo: Ian Tait

Men with Barlow Jackson's plant in 1950. Left to right: Alan Bunt, Bricky Hayes, Barlow Jackson, Herb Huemiller, Ian 'Spud' Tait, Jack Jackson (Jnr) and Claude Burns. Photo: Ian Tait

Trouble with the Cook

During the time I was droving, I often found myself short handed. On one particular trip there were only three of us with 1350 bullocks and 45 head of horses. My brother Jeff did both the cooking and horsetailing jobs, while John Schonrock and I were with the mob. Being so short handed—down three men—made life rather difficult, as each of us had to do a three and a half hour watch each night. This situation continued for about six weeks, and to make matters worse the mob developed contagious bovine pleuropneumonia, a lung disease commonly called just pleuro. As a result, the authorities had to be notified and a stock inspector met me and ran his eye over the mob.

Most drovers regard stock inspectors as a damned nuisance, but I found this bloke, Jack Travers, to be all right. In fact, Jack and I became good mates and have remained so ever since. As a result of his visit, my mob was ordered to stop travelling and was quarantined at the Buchanan River. As he was leaving, I asked Jack if he could find me some men to relieve the situation. He promised to do what he could when he got to Camooweal.

When Jack returned a few days later to check the mob again, he had failed to get me any ringers, but he had brought out a camp cook. He looked like a typical bushman—lean almost to the point of emaciation—but I was to realise later that his physique was due more to a drink-affected liver than to the rigours of outback life. After three days of very indifferent cooking, the new man complained about the lack of rations, which was an accurate enough assessment of the situation. He suggested he catch a ride into Camooweal and bring back some stores, and also mentioned that he knew a couple of ringers who were looking for work. I took him at face value and gave him an open cheque for the goods.

When he hadn't shown up at the end of the third day I began to have misgivings about placing trust in a man I hardly knew. My doubts were confirmed the next day. I cursed myself for a fool when the cook arrived as full as a boot, clutching a bottle of rum. There were no rations and no ringers. I impounded the bottle, and the cook, after staggering around, crashed in his swag. He was still there at sundown, forcing Jeff, who loathed cooking, to knock up a meal for us. Light rain fell early in the night, causing the bullocks to drift off camp, and holding them kept both my brother amd me busy for some time. When things had settled down a little, Jeff rode around to me with a worried look on his face.

'One of us had better go into the camp. The cook is having a fit by the fire.'

'Stuff the cook.'

'Stuff him if you like, but he's likely to roll into the fire.'

I looked at my brother. 'Well, if he does, I hope the bastard burns well—we're short of wood.'

My brother rode away shaking his head. I had not really meant what I said, but felt a great deal better for having said it. When I finally went into the camp, the cook had returned to his swag without augmenting the wood supply.

We started travelling again next day and planned to go out about four miles (6–7 kilometres) after watering the mob. The cook took no part in getting breakfast or in packing up. He looked so close to death that I took pity on him and gave him a stiff rum. I doubt if he would have made it to the next camp without it. As it was, Jeff had to help him onto a horse.

When I put the bullocks on camp that night, the cook was in his swag and Jeff was doing the cooking—and in a foul mood. Next morning the patient looked reasonably fit but refrained from lifting anything heavier than a knife and fork. I got the distinct impression that my brother was beginning to regret that the threatened immolation of the cook had not in fact taken place.

We were crossing the Rankine Plain, a treeless expanse of some 50 kilometres with one bore approximately halfway across. That day I planned to dry day the mob, camping a few kilometres short of the bore. The mob neared the camp as a wild-looking storm approached. I fed the mob along as fast as it was possible, to be close to the camp when it broke. I could see a strange vehicle in the camp but took little notice of it until it was driven along the stockroute road and pulled up opposite the mob, blowing the horn. As I rode over, I could see it was an old ex-army truck with no doors. I could also see the cook sitting in the front seat with the camp rifle acrcss his knees.

'What's up,' I asked as I reined my horse up.

'We're going to kill,' said the cook, who was obviously drunk again.

'Like bloody hell. Can't you see that storm? There's plenty of corned beef left in the packs.'

'It all went bad. I threw it out.'

'Well, go back and bloody well pick it up. We're not killing.'

The cook half fell out of the truck. 'We're going to kill,' he insisted. 'I promised me mate some fresh meat.'

'Tell your bloody mate to take you back to the camp, then roll your swag. You're fired.'

The cook levelled the rifle at me. 'If you won't kill for your men, you miserable mongrel, I'll kill you.'

I had no idea if he was bluffing or not, and did not intend to sit around at point-blank range to find out. Slipping out of the saddle, I ducked under my horse's neck and relieved him of the rifle. As the driver was starting the engine, I stuck my head in the cabin of the truck.

'What the hell do you mean by bringing grog into my camp?'

He jerked his thumb at the cook. 'He told me it was his camp.'

'Well, now you know differently. Get the hell out of here and take this bloody ratbag with you.'

The cook had struggled to his feet and was trying to get back into the truck. I helped him with a none too gentle hand. Once seated, he glared at me. 'What about me wages and me rum?'

The truck took off before I could answer. I sat on my horse and watched the truck head across to the camp. It pulled away again as Jeff returned from watering the horse plant. Still carrying the rifle, I rode back across the Mitchell grass to where the mob was feeding along. Thunder rolled and the bullocks' heads went up as they caught the smell of rain on the storm wind. It would not be an easy night. As I pushed the mob towards the camp, I cursed all cooks, my last one in particular. The only one I could think of as being worse was a character called O'Duff, who once cooked in a Gulf stockcamp.

The Ballad of Dirty O'Duff

I once worked on a run where the old Leichhardt flows,
Where the dark tangled gidgee and snappy gum grows.
We were working all hours, we were mustering fats
From the scrub-covered ridges and silver box flats.
Though the work was no worry, conditions were crook,
For the stockcamp was minus the skills of a cook.

So we gritted our molars and pulled our belts tight,
Each cooking in turn when we finished at night.
But one day to the camp came the old station truck
And it seemed fate had granted a change in our luck,
From the cabin there tumbled a hungover slob,
Who in loud tones advised us, 'Cooking's me job.'

'I believe,' said the wreck, 'things have been a bit rough,
Well, you're in for a change or me name's not O'Duff.'
He was famous, he told us, a cook of repute,
And had gone fifteen rounds with Jack Hassen to boot.
But conditions got worse in the camp just as soon
As this fat reprobate got his hands on a spoon.

For he washed very seldom and smelled like a drain
And he soon had us clutching our stomachs in pain.
He was greasy and slack with a liking to spit
Anywhere, not concerned in the least what he hit.
Now bush babblers at best are a difficult crew
But this fellow was dirty, and dangerous too.

With some awful bait-layers my life has been cursed
But without any question O'Duff was the worst.
Now a stockman's a fellow who'll seldom complain,
He will work like a dog in the heat and the rain,
And the tucker he'll thrive on, as everyone knows,
Is enough to make town people turn up their toes.

But all ringers will bail if you push them enough,
And the end of our tether we reached with O'Duff.
For he gave us the trots and quite often the spews
With his villainous curries and sinister stews.
The insides of his dampers were gluey and raw,
With a crust that would fracture a crocodile's jaw.

'Now don't get downhearted' was all O'Duff said,
'You'll be howling for more when I turn out me bread.'
But disasters in dough were the things that we got,
While the flour bags emptied and tempers grew hot.
First he blamed it on flour, then he blamed it on yeast,
Then he blamed the cold nights as our hunger increased.

'Why this hoon can't boil water,' the head stockman said,
'I'll ride bareback to Bourke if he ever makes bread.'
How we watched him each morn as he gazed in surprise
At inert sullen dough that seemed never to rise,
It would sprawl unrepentant and sometimes it shrank,
Then he'd hurl the whole batch down the steep river bank.

Down the bank every day went the dough that was flat
Until every wild pig on the Leichhardt was fat.
There they'd gather each evening in hoggish delight
And they'd gourmandise loudly far into the night.
In swinish abandon they'd gorge on the stuff,
Their porcine praise swelling to honour O'Duff.

Well, this stirred the head stockman, at last got his goat,
For he sprang from his horse, grabbed O'Duff by the throat.
'You unnatural disaster—you poisonous swine,
Just once more on our bread will your bloody mates dine—
Just once more let them feast and they'll have you, by God,
For I'll strangle you outright, you bait-laying sod.'

Well, our dough roaster spluttered and quickly agreed
That no more feral pigs on his dough would he feed.
We rode campwards that evening with visions of bread,
To be greeted as ever with damper instead.
There we ate with reluctance, no cook was in sight
And no sound of a pig broke the Gulf Country night.

Then we sat around smoking, not caring to talk,
Till the head stockman said he must go for a walk,
For the calls of old nature were sudden enough
On the culinary crimes conjured up by O'Duff.
He had only just left us when rending the air
Came the horrified cry of a soul in despair.

While our flesh crawled, we stood there, aghast and afraid,
Then, fearful hearts thumping, we raced to his aid.
In a monster's foul grip he was trapped to the thighs,
And the grey evil 'thing' seemed to quiver and writhe.
When at last he was freed from his devilish foe,
We found that the 'thing' was a pit full of dough.

But the pigs hadn't dined, O'Duff's promise was sound,
Like a doctor, his failure he'd put in the ground.
And away in the Gulf where the wild Leichhardt flows—
Where the dark tangled gidgee and snappy gum grows—
Where the stockcamps still muster and living is rough,
Many still curse the memory of Dirty O'Duff.

Sam Fuller's Thoroughbrace

Sam Fuller's was a well-known face on stockroutes yesteryear,
And Fuller bought a thoroughbrace to shift his droving gear.
A spanking coach it once had been in days of Cobb and Co.,
That carried mail on roads between the 'Reach and Jericho.
Converted to a wagonette, Sam Fuller thought it grand
Despite the fact he'd still to get a team of five-in-hand.

We loaded on the gear and swags, we roped them into place,
Then culled the plant for likely nags to pull the thoroughbrace.
We draughted five from Fuller's mob, the progeny of sin,
Then readied tackle for the job of breaking outlaws in.
'We're wasting time,' Sam Fuller cried, 'we're shifting camp you know,
We'll have some fun with them un-tried, we'll break 'em as we go.'

The Boss's word was law, of course, somehow the job was done,
We caught each wild, unbroken horse and harnessed every one.
We battled hard to keep control, then placed as Sam decreed
Two snorting brumbies in the pole, three others in the lead.
As ringers held each horse's head—five timebombs all alive,
Sam Fuller turned to me and said, 'They tell me you can drive?'

In shaking hands I took the reins with, 'Steady, whoa there, whoa!'
Then five mad horses hit the chains as Fuller shouted, 'Go!'
At a reckless pace away we sped, the horses running blind—
Escape they knew was up ahead while hell was close behind.
They bolted out towards the track, the bits between their teeth,
The dust and grasses billowed back, the stones flew underneath.

They held to scorn the heavy load, the smoking brakes were spurned
And when we reached the Jundah road we all but overturned.
The Jundah track was fast and dry and faster grew our speed
For not a hope in hell had I of pulling up the lead.
I held the reins in hands that grew white-knuckled with the strain,
As hooves beat out a mad tattoo and gravel fell like rain.

The leaders bowed the spreader bars, with harness all a-flail
They cleared the road of motor cars and scattered them like quail.
The thoroughbraces pitched and rolled, the camp gear rattled free
Like cargo in a clipper's hold that braves the stormy sea.
I rode the wildly swaying seat, one foot upon the brake,
As ringers yelled, 'You've got 'em beat' and galloped in our wake.

We thundered through a flock of sheep, the polers shied in fright,
But Lady Luck chipped in to keep the wagonette upright.
I waited for the pace to ease, I knew it couldn't last,
But still the dusty gidgee trees like phantoms flitted past.
I saw at last the chains go slack beside the heaving flanks
And as I reined the leaders back I said a prayer of thanks.

The weary horses ceased to fear the vehicle at their backs
And with the brake-shoes riding clear they trotted on like hacks.
They swept past distant station roofs and by a stony hill,
With arching necks and drumming hooves now bending to my will.
What seemed at first a hell-bent trip was now a Sunday drive
As sceptre-like I raised the whip above the team of five.

The big wheels sang the same refrain they'd sung in days of yore
With dust clouds following in train and flying heels before.
The 'braces gently rocked the load and oh! but life was grand
When spinning down the Jundah road with Fuller's five-in-hand.
In fancy's flight I rode with men who drove for Cobb and Co.,
Oh! I was young and foolish then but that was long ago.

The bush is not the same today for time has turned the page,
And out Stonehenge and Jundah way trucks roll on every stage
Long gone is Fuller's wagonette—long gone the plunging team,
But memories that linger yet enshroud me like a dream,
Once more I feel the 'braces sway as at a cracking pace
Down distant roads I'm borne away on Fuller's thoroughbrace.

Prizes for Riders

'Prizes for riders and busters for windbags.' Sam Fuller's call to action beckoned loudly as we sat at the back of the hessian-walled buckjump show with the horses. We looked at one another and smiled wryly; Sam was in full flight, drumming up business for the show that was scheduled to start in half an hour. We sat in a rough circle on the ground; Sam didn't waste money on the unnecessary. There was Banjo Hunt, a top rider; a chap named Dawson; myself; and Sam Albury, who fought all comers, to add variety to the show.

'Step up a little bit closer,' Sam roared, 'and you won't be so far away from the best buckjump show in Australia.' He paused for breath. 'Just a few canvas chairs left,' he advised the growing crowd. There was, of course, not a canvas chair to be seen on the inside of the hessian wall, nor, for that matter, was there a chair of any sort. That did not worry Sam. No chairs meant a bigger crowd, for chairs took up space.

Sam Fuller's buckjump show was austere to say the least. A roped ring into which the horses were led was surrounded by a hessian wall, with a reasonable space left for spectators. It was quickly erected and just as quickly pulled down. Sam liked to keep on the move. He had always combined his buckjump show with his droving activities and was not above putting a long flank rope on a plant horse if he thought it had potential. I had been horsetailing for one of his plants, and a big brown horse I had broken in to nightwork had been pressed into service at an earlier show. The horse had acquitted himself well, but every day after that he thought the droving plant was a buckjump show. That night he stood with the other horses, his ears pricked at Sam's spruiking.

Sam Fuller was a hard case and a charismatic character. At one time he drove a taxi in Longreach as well as having two droving plants on the go. A taxi ride with Sam could be an interesting affair. He was not above letting the car idle along in first gear, then, when passing a pub, opening his door and stepping out, leaving his startled passenger to carry on alone. Sam had a rather outrageous sense of humour and could at times get away with acts that would attract censure if perpetrated by others.

The latter part of Sam's life was spent in Longreach, the home of the Stockmans' Hall of Fame. There is, however, no mention of the legendary

Sam Fuller in that august establishment. Perhaps Sam was not polished enough for the 'powers that be' at the Hall.

One of a large family, Sam was born in 1900. After the death of his grandmother in England, Sam's grandfather left the UK and brought his teenage son out to Australia. Before the turn of the century they settled in Mitchell, in the Central West of Queensland. Sam's father grew up and married there, and the town has been 'Fuller' country ever since. As a lad, Sam went bush, and he never looked back. He worked on stations and with drovers, earning a reputation as a buckjump rider. During the 1920s and 1930s he got his own plant together, doing droving and picking up buckjumping horses wherever he could. Sam loved rough horses; it was a passion that stayed with him all his life. He was always ready to turn his droving plant into a buckjump show, for Sam was, above all, a showman. People all over Queensland and various parts of New South Wales have heard the Fuller cry: 'Prizes for riders and busters for windbags.'

People often gave Sam bad horses that were too much trouble to work, and he never knocked them back. In fact, if he took a shine to a buckjumper that was unavailable, he was not above 'borrowing' it. Sam was an accomplished buckjump rider, but he was as rough as guts. His idea of taking the sting out of a bad horse was to leap into the saddle, order the gates open and disappear with a roar and a bellow across whatever terrain happened to be about. When he rode in his show, however, he was professional. He often rode a buckjumper he knew and played the mouth organ in the process—and at times he rode blindfolded.

Sam married Dorrie Zeller in Mitchell in 1920. The couple had four children: three girls—Mabel, Dorrie, and Phillis—and Sam Jnr, the second eldest, who was born in 1925. Mabel died as a result of injuries received in a five-in-hand accident near Dalby. Phillis is also deceased. Dorrie now lives at Caboolture and young Sam, who is now called old Sam, lives at Mitchell. He still rides horses and works in stockcamps. A top horseman, he is made in a different mould to that of his father.

It's probably true to say that Sam Fuller Snr was far from the ideal family man. The lure of the bush and the buckjump show could not be denied. Out there was freedom and excitement, and, above all, buckjumpers. Always on the lookout for horses that he could back to throw anyone, he picked up a horse he called Send Em. Horses that will continue to buck whenever it is asked of them are rare. In Send Em, Sam had a champion. The horse's name became a household word wherever Fuller's show had entertained the public. Sam pensioned off Send Em in New South Wales after taking a mob down there. When I was with him, he had two top buckjumpers, Depot Glen and Wait and See; they were dam and daughter, and a formidable pair.

Later Sam had a little grey horse he called Sugar. The grey would let kids ride him around bareback, but put a saddle and flank girth on him and it was a very different story. It was about this time that the song 'Sugar in the Morning' hit the airwaves. Sam gave that song hell. He sometimes sang another song when I was with him; someone had written it and given the words to him. I'd forgotten it, but while interviewing his son, Sam Jnr, in Mitchell recently, he mentioned the ditty, and after thinking about it for a while, Sam remembered the words. It went like this:

There's hessian walls and a sawdust floor,
With Sam Fuller spruiking at the door,
Pointing the way for us to go
So we found ourselves at the buckjump show.
There's not a seat, for the tent is bare,
But Sam gives a cooee so we don't care.
The side of the hessian wall comes down
And in comes a grey with a mighty bound.
There's prizes for riders here, you know,
For this is Fuller's Buckjump Show.

The very worst thing that can happen in a buckjump show is for a top buckjumper to be ridden right out. This often causes a horse to throw in bucking, making the horse a liability rather than an asset. All showmen are adept at using the long flank rope; if a rider from the crowd looked like riding one of Sam's horses, he usually managed to unseat him by the covert use of this rope. If one of his own men were riding, it was an unwritten law that the rider left the horse before it stopped bucking. I remember Banjo having some great tussles with the two brown mares.

The morning after Sam put on his buckjump show, Banjo Hunt and I were in the bar of the Central Hotel. Banjo had just finished for the season, having been in charge of a packhorse plant of Sam's, and Jimmy Charles and I had been with the other one, using a five-in-hand wagonette.

Sam had been at the hotel entertaining the drinkers with the mouth organ and when he left the crowd had thinned out a bit. We were talking over a quiet beer when out of the blue Banjo looked at me and said, 'How about going down to the Rocky rodeo?'

I was thinking about the suggestion when the barman said, 'You're a bit late. There isn't any accommodation left in Rockhampton, it's the Australian championships, you know.'

Banjo looked at him. 'What! None at all?'

'Nope, not for the public, anyway. I believe they still have some reservations for competitors.'

'Right,' said Banjo, 'Come on, Simmo, we'll nominate.'

'Like hell,' I said. 'I'm no rodeo rider.'

'It's no bloody different. Come on, mate, we'll get a grandstand view of things.'

Banjo could be very persuasive. In the end I agreed and we caught the mail train. In Rockhampton I was to find that Sam Fuller's name could open many doors. As soon as we arrived, we headed for the rodeo office. Rex Pilbeen, the city mayor, was the rodeo boss. He greeted us with: 'What can I do for you chaps?'

Banjo grinned, 'We're here to nominate.'

Pilbeen shook his head. 'Sorry, nominations closed yesterday, and we're not taking late ones.'

Banjo scratched his head. 'Well, we've come all the way from Longreach—we've been with Sam Fuller—and they tell us there's no accommodation left in town.'

Rex's expression changed. 'Oh! You've been with Fuller, eh. Well, I'll tell you what we can do. We're short of a couple of blokes to saddle up on the chutes. It's worth a bit of money plus a room at a pub. Are you interested?'

Were we interested? We both said yes at the same time.

After booking in at the pub, I told Banjo I was going to find a dentist. The rodeo was on next morning and I had a top wisdom tooth that was giving me hell. I reckoned it was best to get it out first. I spent about two hours in the dentist's chair; the tooth broke off and the dentist had to lance the gum to extract the bloody thing. I never got much sleep that night, for it never stopped bleeding. I'd heard George Huntly was the shute boss, so next morning I asked Banjo to tell George I may be a bit late as I was going back to the dentist to get the gum stitched up.

I arrived at the rodeo grounds via a taxi and went straight to the yards. George, who was a big, gruff character, saw me and roared, 'You're late, aren't you supposed to be saddling up here?'

Before I could answer, a chap standing by chipped in, 'He's one of Fuller's men, George.' Again Sam's name worked like magic, and the attitude of the shute boss transformed. He told me I was on chute six and walked off.

I enjoyed the job, for I had a box seat. People pay money and never get as close to the action as Banjo and I were.

I saddled up for Johnny Roberts in the final of the buckjumping. After he was thrown, I witnessed one of the all time great rides; Tom Willoughby won the championship on a big brown horse called Wombi. Both Banjo and I knew we had Sam Fuller to thank for the memorable time we had together in Rockhampton.

After his first wife died, Sam Fuller married again. He wed Ivy Wager in Longreach and the couple were together until Sam's death. The union was blessed with nine children.

Sam Fuller was a living legend of the outback, one of those colourful, larger than life characters that the Australian bush sometimes produces. Love him or hate him, when Sam departed this mortal coil he left a vacuum that has not been filled. Sam died in 1973 and was buried at Longreach.

A Toast to Sam Fuller

Bush horsemen come charge a glass and drink a toast with me,
Though Sam has gone, his name will live, here's to his memory.
His name was known in every camp across this sunlit state,
For all the West was home to Sam, and every man was mate.

Buckjumpers were Sam's very life, his outlaws were his pride,
The eager crowds in countless shows have seen Sam Fuller ride.
How often have we heard him shout, with all the Fuller zest,
There's prizes here for riders, lads, and busters for the rest.

Wherever bushmen's fires are lit beneath a starry sky,
The legend that Sam Fuller left behind will never die.
Whenever horsemen crowd the rails to watch a battle grim
Between an outlaw and a man, they'll think again of him.

A horseman of the old hard school, a showman to the end,
A diamond rough, no doubt, and yet, he never failed a friend.
So horsemen all where'er you are, come drink a toast with me,
Though Sam has gone, his name will live, here's to his memory.

The Take Down

It was just after the horse muster there had begun
That a new chum arrived at the Jabiru run.
From the mail truck he stepped in a bored kind of way
With 'Morning my man' to the boss's 'Good day'.
He was dressed to the nines with immaculate care
From his pigeon-toed feet to his pomaded hair.

From the station's head office in London he came,
And Hector Smythe-Smithers we learnt was his name.
That night after tea for an hour or more
The new chum held forth till our eardrums were sore,
He told of his triumphs at English showgrounds
And of scrub-dashing efforts while 'following hounds'.

He spoke of buckjumpers he'd tamed for a bet
And the rep that he'd won with the show jumping set.
'I suppose they root here,' he remarked, 'but, of course,
A bush nag can't buck like a thoroughbred horse.'
Then the horse breaker said in a muttered aside,
'It's as plain as a pikestaff this dummy can't ride.

'We'll kid him on Blister and drop him a peg,
He's a cert to get thrown if he doesn't renege.'
Now Blister we'd mustered that very same day,
He could buck, twist and spin like a whirlwind at play.
We'd packed him and loaded the packbags with sand,
But the outlaw bucked on till he near threw his brand.

So the head stockman said, 'If you feel like a ride,
We've got a roan horse here that's never been tried,
You could back yourself, sonny, and make a few bob
For they'll bet on a dog fight, this mustering mob.'
The plan was approved by our friend from the town
And we gleefully covered the notes he put down.

For action next morning Smythe-Smithers was keen,
And the clobber he wore was the queerest we'd seen,
He was decked out in jodhpurs and stylish tweed coat
With a polo-necked jumper protecting his throat.
His tall boots, we noted, had heels that were flat
And for head wear he sported a smart bowler hat.

He slapped a smart thigh with a light riding crop
As he strolled to his fate like a chook to the chop.
Then we sat on the rails and prepared for the show
As the horse breaker saddled up Blister below.
He held out the reins as the Pommy climbed down
And walked round the roan like a vaudeville clown.

But he reined up the horse in a manner quite cool
Then quickly and lightly he swung to the 'stool'.
When the air cleared a little to give us a view
Smythe-Smithers was still there, and spurring him too,
We sat round the yard like figures of stone
As the Englishman's yells drowned the squeals of the roan.

For, Pommy or not, he could flaming well ride,
He hit the roan cyclone where'er he saw hide.
His boots raked the dust as the bucking horse chopped
But he sat quite at home till the display had stopped.
Then calmly he picked up the slack of the rein
And stepped to the ground with an air of disdain.

But a horseman's a horseman, no matter how flash,
So we all shook his hand as we paid up the cash,
And the horse breaker said as loudly he sighed
'Young feller, it's true you can certainly ride
And you've taught us a lesson of men and of mounts,
When you're judging a book, it's the story that counts.'

Roughriders of the Bush

Australian bush horsemen have always been regarded as the best in the world. Certainly the length of time that bad horses were used for stock-work was far longer than in any other country. Australian stockmen had a style of riding that was uniquely their own, a style born of long hours in the saddle, which was easy on both horse and rider. Bush horsemen favoured what was called the forward seat; that is, the rider's legs were forward of the girth. They tended to slouch forward, as well, which put their centre of gravity over the horse's wither, the pivotal point when a horse is bucking. This is quite different to the seat of show riders and present-day rodeo riders.

The gun horsemen of the stations and stockroutes were virtually unknown outside the areas in which they worked. They rode horses equally as bad as the worst rodeo horses, and not only did they ride these horses and work them, they did so without pick-up men and ambu-lances standing by. Back in the days when the pastoral industry depended exclusively on horses, large stations often had four or five

hundred broken-in stockhorses. Stockmen, or ringers, as they were called, were given a string of five or six to work, and the whole horse plant, sometimes more than 100 head, was changed a number of times during the stock season. Most of these horses would buck when fresh after a spell. Some would never give up the habit and would test a stockman's skill at any time.

When stockmen yarned around the fire at night, the talk invariably turned to buckjumping horses and the top horsemen of the day. It was an environment that produced numbers of good roughriders, for young chaps endeavoured to emulate the feats of the top men. I first became interested in recording the names of the bush roughriders when I was working in the Gulf. Frank Uhr had written to the *North Queensland Register* listing the best men he had met during his life in the outback. As a lad, I had known Frank Uhr. He must have been a little over 70 years of age then, but still looked every inch a horseman when mounted. From that point I gathered names of gun horsemen from the old timers I met. During the 1940s and 1950s I worked with some outstanding men myself, and was determined, like Frank Uhr, to one day record their names for posterity. For information about many of the men in the list that follows, I have had to depend on the word of others; however, I have complete confidence in their expertise.

Few, if any, of the buckjump riders who stayed in the bush ever received any publicity or recognition. As a result, gathering information on them has been a challenge. Quite a few bush riders did take up rodeo riding, and most of these men are well known. With few exceptions, this chapter concentrates on the unknown bush riders, although I have included some bushmen who rode in the early buckjump shows and were taken under the wing of men like Lance Skuthorpe. As every bushman knows, not all top roughriders were good all-round horsemen, while there are many fine horsemen who were not above their peers when it came to riding buckjumpers. The criteria I have used here is the recognised ability of a man to master really bad buckjumpers, regardless of anything else. Regrettably many fine all-round horsemen have been omitted as a result. To avoid comparison between many horsemen still living, I have restricted the register to the first half of this century and earlier. I recognise this eliminates many fine roughriders, Luke McCall among them. Luke once worked for me and loved all horses, no matter how bad they were. The following register of roughriders is largely of men from

Queensland and the Northern Territory as my appeal for information on horsemen from other States was unfortunately very disappointing; however, I thank those few people who did send me information.

The list of roughriders set out below is neither as complete nor as detailed as I would wish; I believe the job was well worth doing, though. This chapter may not make engrossing reading for city dwellers, but it will create interest, and possibly heated debate, amongst all those who at one time have thrown a saddle on a stockhorse. Any resulting discussion can only throw more light on this long-neglected subject.

Set out below is H.G. 'Frank' Uhr's letter that appeared in the *North Queensland Register* some 50 years ago.

> Mr H.F. Uhr writes: Some time back I noticed in the 'Track' a request for the names of outstanding horsemen, probably you will require the names of professional riders, but I am submitting a list of some whom I have personally contacted during my career as a bushman. These men although not professionals in so far as competition riding is concerned were, nevertheless, first-class horsemen, who could or would ride anything that would stand up, and they were local celebrities in this respect.
>
> Firstly I introduce myself as Herbert George Uhr, now known as Frank Uhr, born at Llewellyn, on the Parramatta River (N.S.W.) on the 8th of March 1858. I came to Queensland in 1876 as a jackaroo on Rannes Station, Rockhampton, with Michael Cunningham. Since then I have travelled all over Queensland and the Northern Territory station country, working in different capacities, I did quite a lot of droving and station stocking, and during my career I managed three stations. It was during this time that I came to know H.A. Redford, the well-known fictitious character of Captain Starlight in 'Robbery Under Arms'. I helped him stock Brunette Downs in the Northern Territory, then belonging to McDonald, Smith and Co. On one occasion my brother and I started from Goulburn with 500 head of stud heifers, travelling them to Cape York Peninsula. We were five months on the road without losing a single beast. Many and varied are my experiences of the cattle country, including wild country, wild horses and cattle, wild men and wild natives. I gave up station work in 1907 settling in Finch Hatton, where I have since resided. It is only six months ago that I gave up riding, for the sole reason that I could not get on a horse without being aided. I can assure you that this hurt me very deeply, as I like horses.

Here is my list of first-class riders: **W. and J. CLAYTON** (Chatsworth Station), **M. LALLY** (Mt. Merlin), **C. TOBIN** (Nornsides), **T. RICHARDSON** (Wickton), **J. DILLON** (St. Fort Cooper), **J. MARSHALL** (Lake Elphinstone), **J. GILLIAM** (Eaglefield), **E. GILLIAM** (Blenheim), **T. STERTCH** and **T. McNEIL** (Wellshot), **A. CHICK** (Fanning Downs), **A. TRIVITON** (Hornetbank), **F. DALEY** (Reedy Springs), **J. DALEY** (Broadwater), **H. WALKER** (St. Helens), **JOE ATKINSON** (Travelling Troupe), **J. BRIDGES** (Riverlee), **P. HEGARTY** (Goolsborough), **D. CRONIN** (Newmarket Sales Yard), **G. GROGGIN** (Sesbania), **W. BAILEY SNR.** (Havilah), **P. SYNOTT**, half caste (Corella Downs), **A. WATT**, blackboy (N.T.), **M. McCALL** (Oxford Downs), **H. ROSS** (Creswell Downs), **J. ROLFE** (Wellshot), **C. ROBSON** (Manuka), **D. BLACK** (Sonoma), **W. BATHAM** (Strathmore), **A. ANDERSON** (Ayrshire).

The names of the bush roughriders below are listed alphabetically, not in order of ability.

Ah Won, Johnny   Top horseman from the Northern Territory.

Baldwin, Snowy   Recognised roughrider in the days of the early buckjump shows.

Bannah, Tom   Top old-time horseman from Charters Towers.

Barber, J.   Recognised as a gun man in the Gulf.

Bargo, Billy   An Aborigine from North Queensland. A top roughrider who later joined the early buckjump shows.

Barron, Jack   A top man around the turn of the century, reported to have ridden Dargan's Grey at Clermont in 1906.

Brady, 'Boomerang' Jack   A renowned roughrider in Queensland and the Northern Territory, Brady is buried beside the stockroute on Eva Downs.

Bell, 'Pincher'   A top Gulf horseman, said to have ridden a station outlaw without disturbing coins placed between his boots and the stirrups irons.

Bignell, Paddy   A great roughrider, who worked on Dalgonally.

Brennan, Jimmy   A top buckjumper from the Cooper.

Butterworth, Alf   A top man on a bad horse, from the Nebo district.

Bussy, Charlie   Well-known roughrider in the Nebo area.

Bustard, Bob   A great horseman from Croydon area before the turn of the nineteenth century.

Button, Bob A great roughrider and pioneer of the Kimberley region. In 1884 managed Ord River for Nat Buchanan.

Camilleri, Paul A top horseman from North Eton.

Cant, Sammy A horse breaker and good buckjump rider.

Casey, Leo Casey broke-in on A.P. Company stations for many years, a good man on a bad horse.

Caton, Paddy, Billy and Jim Were all members of a well-known family in the early days in the Stanthorpe district. They had the reputation of being able to ride anything wrapped in hide and often rode the best horses in travelling buckjump shows. Jim, the last of the roughriding family to pass away, served in both world wars.

Clark, Sandy A top horseman from the Mitchell area.

Cleary, Cammy Recognised as the best buckjump rider of his day, Cammy was a balance rider. I worked with him on Alexandria Station, and he was pretty to see on a bad horse.

Clines, Johnny Clines was reputed to be a top roughrider and horse breaker.

Club, Jack A top buckjump rider, Jack was an Aborigine and worked on Ardmore and Oban Stations in the Mount Isa area.

Coleman, Charley A highly regarded Queensland buckjump rider.

Combango, Henry An Aborigine and a great roughrider of the early days. He worked around Surat.

Coomber, Rod Coomber had the reputation of being a top man on a bad horse.

Cotton, Jacky Also known as 'Yellow Jacky', Cotton was an Aborigine who worked on Brunette for many years.

Cowan, Vic A fine bushman and roughrider from Leongatha, Victoria. He worked on stations in New South Wales and Queensland, and rode in buckjump shows in the 1920s.

Coye, Andy Well known around Dimbulah as a top rider.

Craigie, Joe A top man from the Channel Country.

Crisp, Mick Regarded by all as a fine roughrider.

Curley, Bob A fine roughrider from the Gulf Country.

Cusack, Paddy Well known in the Cloncurry district as a top man on a bad horse.

Dale, Splinter A well-known horseman of the Central West.

Dally, Jack Regarded as a fine roughrider in the early part of the twentieth century. He worked in both Queensland and the Northern Territory.

Cammy Cleary.

Daly. An Aborigine who worked on Humbert River Station. According to the late Charlie Schultz, Daly was unthrowable.

Darcy, Charlie Darcy was a great horseman who owned Koonbook Station on Skull Creek in the Kimberley.

Davidson, Cecil A top horseman, Davidson was a head stockman on Gulf stations for many years.

Davis, Frank A top roughrider, he rode an outlaw on Iniskillen Station in 1945 in a saddle without kneepads.

Dawson, Freddy A renowned buckjump rider, Dawson was an Aborigine from the Taroom district.

Diamond, Mick An Aboriginal man, Mick tracked and found alive a small boy who had been lost for two days on Riverslea Station. Mick worked in the Gulf Country, and according to Les Huddy, a top man himself, Mick was not thrown in the 30 years he knew him.

Dixon, Jack A top horseman from the Channel Country.

Dodd, Tommy A highly respected Aborigine and a top horseman, well known in the Territory.

Douglas, Frank (Snr) Well known in the Cloncurry district.

Dowling, 'Looking Glass' Joe A top man on a bad horse, Looking Glass worked in the Gulf Country and was later a Northern Territory boss drover.

Doyle, Bartle A top horseman and buckjump rider, well known on many Gulf stations.

Drenin, Tommy A good man on a bad horse, Drenin was head stockman in the Tambo district.

Duncan, Alex A good man on a bad horse, from the Mitchell district.

Duncan, Colin Alex's brother and a top man on a buckjumper.

Emmerson, Billy Listed by Gregory Mitchell as a top man.

Farber, Harry Farber was born near St Laurence in Queensland in 1879. His father was from Morocco. Farber worked for a number of years on Waverley Station at Broadsound, earning the reputation of being a fine

Frank Douglas Snr.

'Looking Glass' Joe Dowling. Photo: Mrs Ada Devereaux

horseman who was virtually unthrowable when riding bareback. He rode many of the best buckjump show horses using this method. In 1911 he helped overland a mob of 250 horses from the Queensland Gulf to Derby in the Kimberley. There he followed horse breaking and later went droving with a plant of mules. Farber's reputation as a roughrider was enhanced by his work in the West.

Findlay, 'Fin' A top all-round horseman, well known in the Camooweal district.

Finlay, Ross Top rider, from the Thargomindah area.

Fortune, 'Monkey' Fortune had the reputation in the North-West of being a good man on a bad horse.

Fowler, Jim Fowler was head stockman on Alexandria, where he once rode a notorious station outlaw. Later owned and ran the Rankine store.

Fuller, Sam (Snr) A legendary buckjump rider and showman, known throughout Queensland.

Gaiter, Bob Well-known horseman of the Central West.

Grey, Phillip A top horseman from Manilla, New South Wales, broke in horses for 'Bluey' Buchanan in 1880.

Groom, Jim A top man who worked on Dalgonally and Lake Nash.

Harris, Doug A good roughrider and the best all-round horseman I worked with.

Harrison, John Reputed to be a top man on a bad horse.

Hawkins, 'Queensland Harry' An Aborigine and a top roughrider, Harry later travelled with Skuthorpe.

Hayden, Alex Often described as the best of all Aboriginal horsemen. Born at Chinchilla, Hayden won many buckjump championships. He was accidentally killed in the cattle camp on Auburn Station. He was just 34 years old.

Hayes, Jack Said by many to be a good roughrider.

Hill, Billy According to men I have spoken to, Hill was a top rider.

Hill, Sammy Looked after Herbert Downs for many years, few men better on a bad horse.

Horrigan, Jack Jack was head stockman on Kyabra Station in the 1870s. A top roughrider in his youth.

Huey, John Well known around Kynuna, Huey rode the outlaw Windamere Whirlwind.

Hughs, Alex A top horseman, reputed to have undone both saddle girth and bridle while riding a buckjumper.

Hutching, Bob Said to be an excellent roughrider. He worked in the Croydon district as horse breaker.

Hutley, Jack Well-known Gulf horseman.

Hyland, Tom Listed by Gregory Mitchell as a top man.

Isles, Bill, George and Lloyd Members of a well-known Central West Queensland family, all top horsemen.

Johnson, Watty A top man, he managed Bulloo Downs.

Jones, 'Galloping Jack' Well-known Gulf identity and top horseman, a wild character and notorious poddy dodger.

Jungualla I worked on Alexandria when Jungualla was a child. He later worked on other Tableland stations and was regarded as a top roughrider.

Kelly, Pat A well-known horseman who worked in the Barcaldine area of Queensland.

Kerry, Jack A top man on a rough horse, from the Central West of Queensland.

King, Dick A top rider and head stockman in the Queensland Gulf.

Kirkman, Arthur One of the best roughriders in the Gulf Country, he was head stockman on Dalgonally for many years before World War II. After war service he did not return to the North.

Lawton, Fred A top man from the Dawson River area.

Lawton, George A top roughrider, and a member of the Lawton family from Dawson Valley.

Lawton, Ted Another of the Lawtons from Juanda Run in the Dawson Valley, Ted was a top horseman and cattleman.

Ledgerwood, Jim Renowned buckjump rider, well known in the Territory.

Lewis, Elmore Head stockman on Newcastle Waters, and a good roughrider, Lewis was a strong man and a grip rider.

Lewis, George 'Spear Grass' Head stockman on Brunette Downs for many years, and later managed Victoria River Downs. Top all-round horseman.

Lloyd, Leo and Tom (Jnr) Sons of Tom Senior's second marriage. Both were champion buckjump riders who joined Thorpe McConville's troupe of roughriders.

Lloyd, Ned A son of Tom Lloyd and Margaret, Ned Lloyd was regarded as Australia's best buckjump rider in his day. He represented Australia in England in 1911 and later he was with McConville's buckjump show.

Lloyd, Tom (Snr) Tom Lloyd was a cousin of the Kellys and a great horseman in the early days in Victoria. He enjoyed a long and fruitful relationship with Margaret, Kelly's sister after her marriage broke up. Years later, after Margaret died, he married Steve Hart's sister.

Long, George Long was an Aborigine and a top man on a bad horse. He worked in Western Queensland.

Tom Lloyd Jnr. Photo: Mrs Lola Rowe

Longwell, Ray A top horseman who worked in the Central West after World War II. He rode a station outlaw at Oondoroo.

McCall, Ainslie 'Chum' A top man on a bad horse, well known in the Nebo District. 'Chum' was a nephew of Martin McCall, who was listed by Frank Uhr.

McCormac, Billy An Aborigine born at Chatsworth Station, north of Boulia. A top man on a bad horse, Billy later worked as a teamster. He

Tom Lloyd Snr. Photo: Mrs Lola Rowe

Ainslie 'Chum' McCall. Photo: Linda Craig

once took a wagon team to Longreach and while there rode every horse in a buckjump show. Billy died at Kajabbi, Queensland in the mid-1920s.

McHugh, Jim Jim had the reputation of being a fine roughrider. He worked on Clive Station, Marlborough.

Jim McHugh. Photo: Jeff Simpson

McHugh, Mick Like his brother Jim, Mick was recognised as a top man on a bad horse.

McMillan, Les A fine horseman and buckjump rider from the Dawson Valley, McMillan represented Australia overseas.

McPhee, Harry A top horseman from Scone, ex-POW.

Maher, Clarrie 'Chips' A top horseman from the Barcaldine district.

Man Fong, George A fine horseman from the Top End.

Minague, Paddy A famous horseman in the Gulf Country prior to the turn of the nineteenth century.

Morey, Ted A fine all-round horseman and roughrider. Later a well-known member of the Northern Territory mounted police.

Morrissey, Jack Jack came from Grafton in New South Wales, a top bush buckjump rider. With other Australians he rode at Crystal Palace, England in 1911. He travelled with Thorpe McConville.

Murray, Jack A top horseman in the early days, Murray travelled with Thorpe McConville's buckjump shows.

Nagee, Tom A top man from the Beaudesert area.

Nathan, Byron Born on Carrandotta, where his father was speared by Aborigines, Byron had the reputation of being not only good on a bad

Byron Nathan.

horse, but a fine all-round horseman. He worked in both Queensland and the Northern Territory. An Aborigine and expert tracker, he once tracked a pair of cattle duffers for the police. This did not enhance his popularity with his peers.

Nicholson, Don A top rider who worked in the Hughenden and Maxwelton districts during the 1920s.

Ninus, John A top rider, he was head stockman on Mount Howard.

Noble, Bobby A top horseman who worked on Caldervale and other Western Queensland stations.

Noble, Paddy Brother of Bobby Noble and also a good man on a bad horse.

Norman, Tommy An Aborigine who worked on Nockatunga and many other stations in the area, Norman was regarded as one of the best buckjump riders in the Channel Country.

Pattell, Norm Recognised as a top man on a bad horse, he worked in the Cloncurry/Julia Creek area.

Patterson, John An Aborigine and a top horseman, he did a lot of horse breaking on Gulf Country runs.

Pendergast, Jack An early roughrider from New South Wales.

Pendergast, 'Splinter' A top man on a bad horse, well known as a Northern Territory drover.

Pidgin, Roy A well-known buckjump rider from Queensland.

Primus, Noel A very good man on a bad horse. I knew Noel when he was head stockman on Chatsworth Station, Boulia.

Prosser, Tommy Well known for years in the Mount Isa area as a good man on a bad horse.

Richardson, Les Reputed to be a top man on a bad horse.

Rideout, Jack A famous buckjump rider from the Dawson Valley.

Rose, Joe Rose, an Aborigine, was born and reared on Tobermorie Station near Unandangie, Queensland. He was a fine roughrider and rode Strike, an outlaw, in a travelling buckjump show.

Roy, Tommy A fine roughrider, Roy was killed when a horse fell with him.

Rudd, Les Reputed to be a good buckjump rider, Rudd worked in the Gulf Country.

Ryder, Jack A top horseman from the Injune district. Ryder once rode an outlaw—a chestnut horse that had thrown many top professional riders—in the Mitchell showgrounds. He gave the £30 he won to the ambulance.

Tommy Norman. Photo: Mick Bailey

Saltner, Nelson A well-known horseman from the Dawson River, Nelson broke in mounts for the light horse during World War I.

Sherwin, Jack Jack was head stockman on Millungera for many years. He tied his irons on a bad horse.

Simpson, Don A top horseman who worked in the Dawson Valley, Simpson later ran camps at Carpentaria Downs and Forrest Home. At

'Splinter' Pendergast. Photo: the late Bill Yeomans

a remount depot in England during World War I, he rode an outlaw in a bare military saddle.

Simpson, Tom A top horse breaker and rider from the Hunter River District.

Snieder, Charlie Reputed to be a good man on a bad horse.

Snowy An Aborigine from Humbert River and a top man on a bad horse, a brother of Daly.

Southee, Bob A fine roughrider from the Darling Downs, said to have ridden Queenslander, a horse with a big reputation, in a buckjump show.

Speedy, Mick (Snr) A very smart old-time buckjump rider and athlete from Central West Queensland.

Stace, Octavius A good roughrider, Stace worked on stations on Cape York Peninsula during the 1920s and 1930s.

Straton, Wally Straton possibly originally came from South Australia, and worked on stations in Western Queensland. While on Riverdale Station, he rode a black station outlaw. Bob Isles witnessed the display. A top horseman himself, Bob said it was one of the best rides he had ever seen.

Streak, Jack Reported to be a top buckjump rider.

Sullivan, Jack (Snr) One of the best buckjump riders in the Top End. It is said that there was $4000 for many man who could produce a horse that could throw Sullivan.

Symes, Darky A well-known horseman in the Cloncurry/Boulia areas, Symes worked on Warenda as both horse breaker and head stockman. Later was a boss drover.

Taylor, Lou Worked in the Cloncurry district in the 1930s. A great horseman.

Thomas, Ben A good roughrider, Thomas managed Ticlara.

Thomas, Billy 'The Galloping Ghan' A well-known character in Western Queensland, a very good horseman.

Timmins, George A good man on a bad horse and a top man with wild cattle.

Treffett, Ted A top roughrider from the Julia Creek district.

Trimble, Louis Worked in the Einasleigh district during the 1920s. A top man on a bad horse.

Victor An Aborigine from the famous Elsey Station, Victor was a top buckjump rider and a very smart man with a bad beast.

Vitnal, Jack A good roughrider, Vitnal worked in Queensland and the Northern Territory. A grip rider, he was a good man with a bad beast.

Waite, Billy An Aborigine originally from the Gulf Country, he was one of the smartest horseman and showmen of his day. Waite became Skuthorpe's right-hand man and represented Australia more than once in both England and America.

Watson, Jack An Aborigine from Gatton in Queensland, Watson was a top buckjump rider who won a world championship in Sydney in 1924. He later travelled overseas with Skuthorpe.

Weiber, Jack 'Hoot' Reputed to be a very good man on a bad horse.

Werriban, Jack Originally from New South Wales, he was a very smart all-round horseman. Another fine Aboriginal buckjump rider and an expert with scrub cattle. Well known around Surat.

Williams, Johnny Known as 'Yellow Johnny', he was one of the smartest horsemen in Western Queensland. Williams was born at Davenport Station and worked on many outback runs.

Wilson, Jim A top rider from the St George district.

Wilson, Stan An outstanding horseman from Central Queensland.

Wolfe, Roy Originally from Wellshot in Queensland, Wolfe worked in the Northern Territory. A very good man on a rough horse.

Stan Wilson. Photo: Rod Bellette

The above horsemen were the cream of Australia's bush buckjump riders. Few of them ever sought publicity, yet they were perhaps the best roughriders in the world. We should remember them with pride.

Mick Casey

Mick Casey was a drover bloke way out at Whistle Stop
Who never knew the price of meat in any butcher's shop;
For Casey scorned the flaccid steak upon the butcher's shelf
And from the Gillgai Station herd he simply helped himself.
The Gillgai herd was rolling fat—and Gillgai rump was sweet,
Mick Casey and his mates in town were never short of meat,
He always got his beef at night, long practice lent him speed,
The stars alone looked down and saw Mick Casey do the deed.

To cattlemen and police alike Mick Casey was a thief,
But many thought it not a crime to dine on station beef.
The Gillgai run was English owned and runs like this it's true
Have long been used by larrikins to boost their revenue.
A sergeant came to Whistle Stop, a cunning sort of bird,
He learnt of Casey's barbecues and fumed at what he heard;
He made a promise then and there that justice would prevail,
And loudly swore he wouldn't rest till Casey was in jail.

Mick Casey laughed at idle threats, not bothered in the least
He sharpened up his butcher's knives to kill another beast.
And just to show he held no grudge towards the local law
He left a juicy sirloin roast beside the sergeant's door.
The status quo remained intact, as days and weeks went by
With Casey eating fillet steak—the sergeant, humble pie.
For Casey kept his fridge well stocked as he was wont to do,
Till fickle fate and carelessness brought on his waterloo.

One night he killed by Gillgai Creek and after he had gone
He cursed himself, remembering he'd left the earmark on,
That in itself was bad enough, then driving back through town
Just as the dawn began to break, his trusty ute broke down.
When evening came to Whistle Stop and light began to fail
The sergeant's fridge was full of meat, with Casey out on bail.
They found the carcass with the head and quickly cut it loose,
This Gillgai head, the sergeant said, will really cook his goose.

They placed it in a drum of brine behind the station cells,
To pickle it until the trial and neutralise the smells.
Mick Casey kept his spirits up, despite the loss of face,
But sausages were all the go for meals at Casey's place.
The breaker came to town one night, he laughed when he was told,
'Some action here is what you need, a simple plan and bold,
I reckon I can help you mate, because I know you well
For twenty quid I'll pinch the head and blow the case to hell.'

The deal was struck, the money paid, the breaker grabbed a sack.
'Go down the creek and dig a hole, wait there till I get back.
There's shelter there, so light a fire, and take some Bundy rum,
I'll signal you if all is clear, I'll whistle as I come.'
The breaker travelled through the dark avoiding any light,
His movements were as furtive as kadaicha men at night.
He reached the lock-up fence at last, he froze at every sound,
Then silently he crossed the yard, his belly to the ground.

The breaker slid the cover back and reaching through the scum
He grasped a horn and slowly drew the head out of the drum.
He heaved the bag onto his back returning without pause,
Mick Casey saw him coming like an outback Santa Claus.
They buried deep the evidence in hope that crime might pay,
Then Casey opened up the rum and threw the cork away.
On Friday Casey faced the court but Casey's step was light,
No longer did the threat of jail hang o'er him like a blight.

A magistrate to hear the case from down the line was brought,
And all of Whistle Shop turned out when Casey went to court.
They lugged inside the heavy drum and with it came as well
The subtle scent of Casey's crime—a faint accusing smell.
But Casey stood there in the dock quite certain of his fate,
When asked to plead he gave a grin. 'I didn't do it mate.'
The sergeant gave the facts, then said, 'Your Worship, if I may,
Draw your attention to the drum that's marked "Exhibit A".

'It holds the Crown's best evidence, a most important clue,
For in it rests a bullock's head—the one that Casey slew.'
The sergeant walked up to the drum, he drew the cover off,
Mick Casey made a strangled sound that ended as a cough.
The sergeant rolled his shirt sleeves up, he paused as show men do,
Then plunged his bare arms elbow deep into the sluggish brew.
He fished around inside awhile, the court was hushed with dread,
Then from the drum he lifted high a Gillgai bullock's head.

This sergeant was a wily bird, when all is said and done,
It's common knowledge that two heads are better than just one.
He'd checked the drum the day before, but nothing had been said,
He simply shot another beast and got another head.
Mick Casey looked across the court in utter disbelief,
And realised the police had sent a thief to catch a thief.
'I'll change me plea,' Mick Casey groaned. 'And cop what comes me way,
For there's a smarter rogue than me in this here court today.'
Though Casey sweats in durance vile to pay for what he did,
The thing that galls him most of all is wasting twenty quid.

Characters and Hard Cases

The eccentric behaviour and idiosyncrasies of outback characters have seldom raised an eyebrow; nevertheless, I remember a few cases whose bizarre habits placed them in a class of their own.

Years ago an elderly character known as Sully was employed as a station cook on Sudan, an outstation of Alexandria. As the stockcamp was out on the run most of the time, Sully acted as caretaker as well as cook, a dual role that he relished. It must be said that Sully took his responsibilities very seriously and this, coupled with an intense dislike of his fellow man, caused the welcome he extended to visitors to be rather less than that demanded by bush hospitality.

Sully's constant companion was a half-naked cockatoo that appeared to be permanently fixed to his left shoulder. On meeting Sully for the first time, a keen observer might arrive at two conclusions: firstly, the cockatoo always faced the front; and secondly, Sully seldom if ever changed his shirt—the back of the garment was thickly encrusted with cockatoo droppings. Although Sully was entirely without teeth, he constantly chewed tobacco. You needed to be on your toes when you were around him, for he expelled the juice from his pursed lips with more velocity than accuracy. Like the cockatoo, Sully was a bit thin on top and what hair he did have he cropped short, giving him the appearance of an old lag.

Sully had his own method of discouraging outside visitors. He would emerge from the kitchen with a skinning knife in one hand, a butcher's steel in the other, and the cockatoo on his shoulder. Both he and the bird would fix the stranger with an unblinking stare, then, gently caressing the steel with the knife, Sully would ask in a hoarse whisper, 'Did anyone see you come here?'

No matter what the visitor said in reply, Sully's rejoinder was always the same: 'Well, no one is going to see you leave.'

It invariably worked; Sully and the cockatoo would return to the kitchen in triumph as the caller departed in a cloud of dust.

Years ago a well-known Gulf station was managed by a colourful figure who at times got a bee in his bonnet and sacked the whole station staff. At that time the mail truck ran down the Leichhardt River to

Burketown on one day and returned the next. One morning when the mail was due and all hands were in at the homestead, the manager walked into the men's dining room at breakfast time and sacked everyone, including the cook. They got their cheques from the bookkeeper and in due course climbed onto the mail truck.

That evening the manager and the bookkeeper sat down to a frugal repast prepared by the bookkeeper. After the meal, the bookkeeper leaned back in his chair. 'Well, Mr . . ., there's only you and me left now.'

'That's true,' replied the manager, 'and after the mail truck leaves tomorrow, there will only be me.'

One old-time Territory drover, who was well liked and respected by his peers, was very hard on himself. He had a violent temper, but he seldom directed his spleen at anyone but himself. He usually had a large wagonette on the road with him and used the vehicle in a unique way to punish himself for perceived mistakes. Removing his hat, he would stand back and then charge head-down into a wagonette wheel. After he had regained his feet, he would replace his hat and declare, 'Well, that will knock a bit of sense into you.'

The wagonette was a large one, enabling the drover to carry packs in case of the vehicle breaking down. On one occasion he reached camp to find he had lost one of a pair of water canteens. A packsaddle carries one canteen on each side, to balance the load. One canteen, then, is as useful as a hip pocket in a singlet. The drover roared and raged, then, unable to restrain himself any longer, he grabbed the camp axe and laid into the odd canteen. He had just finished belting it into a mass of twisted metal when a station vehicle pulled by the camp with its missing mate. Once again the drover was left with an odd canteen. It was just too much. Roaring and swinging the axe, he charged the second canteen as the startled motorist leapt behind the wheel of his vehicle and fled. After the drover had disembowelled the object of his wrath, he pulled off his hat and gave the wagonette wheel a touch up.

The indigenous people of the Northern Territory have suffered greatly from diseases introduced by Macassar seafarers and whites. During World War II the influx of both American and Australian forces to the Northern Territory caused a serious increase in venereal disease. This outbreak proved to be as big a threat to the white 'combos' (white men who lived with Aboriginal women) as it did to the Aborigines. However, penicillin, the magic bullet, soon had the disease under control, and the combos took the malady in their stride. There was actually a joke among these hardened sinners that a man had to have suffered from what they called 'the pox' before he made the grade. One old reprobate I knew used to introduce himself with these words: 'They say a bloke has to have had the pox once before he's a man. Well, shake hands with Superman.'

In the days when the horse was still king, outback cooks were an eccentric lot who were sometimes rather unreliable. A fine exponent of camp-oven cuisine was a character known as Barefoot Bob. As the name implies, he never wore boots, and his feet had calluses on them like those of a camel. Barefoot Bob cooked for me on one droving trip and I found him one of the best packhorse cooks I'd struck; nothing was any trouble for Barefoot Bob. Most cooks on the road will only pack the horse carrying the cooked tucker pack. Barefoot Bob, though, would get stuck into throwing on as many packs as the horsetailer. When working around the fire, he sometimes stood on a live coal; someone would have to tell him, for the smell of burning skin pervaded the camp long before Barefoot Bob felt any pain.

I first met the barefooted cook when I was working on Alexandria. Bob was doing the cooking and got on well with us all. During a few days spell at the Rankine, someone dared Barefoot Bob to walk across a huge pile of broken bottles at the back of the place. Fortifying himself with OP rum, he faced up to the challenge, then marched across singing 'Onward Christian Soldiers'. He did not suffer as much as a scratch.

That night Barefoot Bob, flushed with victory and rum, fell asleep by the open campfire. I'm not sure what woke me, but I looked up to see our cook ablaze from the knees down. Leaping out of my swag, I threw a handy bucket of water over him. Next morning Barefoot Bob seemed more concerned about his ruined trousers than about any burns he had suffered.

There was one character who had worked on the same Gulf Country station for many years. Sometimes he was employed as the station cook and at other times he did the cowboy's job; that is, milk the cows and chop the wood etc. This character, who we will call Jim, had a great weakness for rum and often, to the manager's chagrin, became a real nuisance. One Anzac eve Jim and a mate secured a bottle of Bundy from sources unknown and proceeded to make the station buildings echo with their revelry. No one had a chance of getting any sleep, and about midnight the manager decided that enough was enough and strode down to the men's quarters. He threw open the door of Jim's room to see the pair standing to attention as the Last Post was played at the midnight service. Disregarding the show of patriotism, the manager tore a strip off them both, and sacked Jim on the spot.

Next morning the head stockman was at the horseyards. He had heard the night's barney from the next room and was surprised to see Jim, as usual, milking a cow, his head buried in her flank. He strolled over and addressed the hungover cowboy.

'I thought you got the sack last night.'

'Oh,' replied Jim, 'if I took any notice of that baldy-headed bastard I'd never have a job.'

There was a stockman known as 'Ding Dong' Bell who worked on stations over quite a lot of Queensland. Ding Dong was a bit of a character, and a bit of a nutcase as well. He often complained about entities he called 'Nigly Aglies' that hassled him. Despite this aberration, Ding Dong was an excellent stockman. I never worked with him myself, but more than once have had a drink with him. He did at times, however, do some crazy things, including burning down his mother's house. Ding Dong finally overstepped the boundary of eccentricity when he decapitated a chap with a cane knife.

The greatest group of hard cases to ride north to the Territory was, without doubt, the notorious Ragged Thirteen. Their exploits have become part of the folklore of the North, and time may well have enhanced their reputation for devilry. Nevertheless, the thirteen were a formidable lot who made free with the stock and property of those unlucky enough to be in the wrong place at the wrong time. The Ragged Thirteen didn't embrace any romantic notions about robbing from the rich to give to the poor, but no one left their camp hungry. Despite their depredations, Territorians never really regarded the Ragged Thirteen as criminals. Whenever I heard them mentioned, it was more with admiration than antipathy. The group apparently got its name from one of their number, 'Tommy The Rag'. According to legend, Rag's thirteen was corrupted to become the 'Ragged Thirteen'.

They were tough men in a land where only the tough survived. All good horsemen, most of them would just as soon have a fight as a feed. The group rode through the Territory heading for the goldfields around Hall's Creek. Some struck it lucky and some didn't. I was privileged to meet a few of them in later life. The leader of the Ragged Thirteen, Tom Nugent, changed his name and established Banka Station, north of Tennant Creek. Another, Bob Anderson, battled droughts and low prices on Tobermory, a run over the border fence, west of Boulia. Anderson is buried on Tobermory and the station is still owned by the family. The rest of them scattered to the four winds, but the legend of the Ragged Thirteen remains.

Otto Khan was a rather benign character who kept a drovers' store at Urandangie. What set him apart from his fellows was his race. Otto was an Afghan, a cameleer who, like his countrymen, turned his hand to other things when the humble camel had had its day. He had a lively sense of humour and wasn't above having a joke with the stockmen and drovers. He met his match when he greeted Jimmy Carr with the words: 'Ah! Jimmy Carr, all the same as motor car.'

'Yes,' replied Jimmy, 'and you're Otto Khan, black as a billy can.'

Otto Khan liked to get fresh meat from the drovers whenever they killed close to the town. However, his religion forbade the eating of meat unless the beast was killed in a manner dictated by the code of Islam. Anyone could shoot the selected beast, but they then had to stand back while Otto Khan bled the carcass and offered up a halal prayer. That done, the meat was cut from the carcass and Otto went off happily with his share.

James Francis 'Gidgea' Taylor was one of the great characters of Winton in outback Queensland. Born in 1905, he suffered from poor eyesight and a slight disability, whether from birth or from a childhood disease like measles is not recorded. Whatever the cause, Gidgea did not let it bother him. He went on to become a much loved character of the town. From a very young age Gidgea was the mascot of the Winton Rugby League team, leading the players on to the field at every home and away game. His memory of past matches was phenomenal. He could quote results and scores of football games going back many years, and could name the winners of any major horse race. Because of his eyes, he never learnt to read or write. Nature must have compensated for this by giving him an almost infallible memory. He only had to hear some detail and it stayed with him forever.

Another of Gidgea Taylor's claims to fame was that he was probably the last town crier in Queensland. Bill Evert, who owned the Royal Theatre, paid Gidgea a retainer to act as a town crier to advertise coming attractions. Gidgea, complete with bell, patrolled the streets of Winton. His description and commentary on the expected movies was at times more entertaining than the films. Gidgea often rode a bike when running messages for the Winton Hotel, where he was an odd job man. It was a common sight to see him pedalling back to the pub with parcels balanced on his head. At age 18 he is reported to have won a bravery award for rescuing a lad from drowning in the Winton dam. In the early 1950s Gidgea Taylor was presented with a Winton Rugby League blazer in honour of his service to the club.

As he grew older and his eyesight became worse, he gave up the bike and walked everywhere. He learned to recognise people by their voices: once heard never forgotten. Gidgea could recognise anyone who had previously spoken to him. Gidgea Taylor died in 1965 and was buried in his football blazer. He is remembered by those who knew him as a great character and a true blue Aussie.

Brian Rezes really was a hard case. He was a big, genial character with an infectious chuckle and an acknowledged weakness for strong drink. After working on wages as a stockman for some time, Brian had a stroke of luck. His uncle, a well-respected drover, gave Brian a complete droving plant to start him off on a career as a boss drover. Brian did a couple of trips, then got on the grog at the Urandangie pub. He drank his cheque then started on the plant. Saddles, horses and packs were all sold, and the money went over the bar. What his uncle thought of this is not known. Having liquidated his assets, Brian was forced to go back working for wages. He ended up cooking in the Channel Country stockcamps. Brian's specialty was cooking fritters, called 'Burdekin Ducks' in the bush; Brian called his 'Rezes' scrumpducks', although the scrumptious prefix was open to debate. Brian passed on well before his time. He was on a spree in Winton and went to sleep on the lawn between two pubs. He never woke up. For a man who had drunk a whole droving plant, it was an apt place to depart for the last muster.

Albert James 'Tie Wire' Edwards was not so much a hard case as a hard man. When a boss drover, he was refused water from a station owner when the mob he was in charge of were badly in need of a drink. Edwards offered to pay for the water but again met with a blunt refusal. Now, a boss drover is judged by the condition of the cattle he delivers, and Edwards was not about to jeopardise his reputation. Grabbing the station manager by the scruff of the neck, Edwards took him over to a tree, where he effected the immobilisation of his captive by tying him to the tree with a piece of tie wire across the bridge of his nose. Having neutralised the opposition, Edwards proceeded to water his mob. In due course he released the blaspheming owner, who swore he'd have Edwards's guts for gaiters.

He did sue the drover, and the case went to court. There must have been some good cattlemen on the jury, for Edwards was acquitted. From then on he was known as 'Tie Wire' Edwards. He later became a manager for Kidman.

Thomas Anzac Burrows was an outstanding character. It was not that Tom was an eccentric or a ratbag; he was simply a character, and a likeable and unique one at that. As a teenager he suffered terrible injuries when a horse fell with him. After weeks in a coma, he regained consciousness and left hospital to face life with a serious handicap. To say that Tom overcame that handicap would be an understatement. His sheer guts and determination won him respect and a large number of friends. Tom never lost his sense of waggish humour. More than once I have seen him turn a situation that was about to become serious into one of laughter.

The Glengyle mustering camp at Pulchera yard on the Mulligan River, early 1920s. A.J. 'Tie Wire' Edwards is in white with arms folded. Photo: lent by Blue Ellis

Tom was on the road droving with me not long after his accident. On the way out to pick up cattle, we ran into a rat plague. That night we camped at a government bore and hung all the packs and packbags up in trees to prevent the rats devouring them. It looked like being a sleepless night, but Tom had other ideas.

'Sleep in your swags,' he told us. 'I'll guard the camp tonight.'

We wondered what he was up to, but soon all was revealed. Getting a long length of number eight wire from the fence around the bore, he doubled it then twisted the two halves together.

'This', he said, swishing it about, 'is what I call Tom's tranquilliser. No rodent will enter this camp tonight.'

We unrolled our swags and watched with interest. Tom built up a large fire, threw out a piece of corned meat as bait, then sat down with his tranquilliser across his knees. The action was not long in coming; throughout the night our sleep was broken by the sounds of swish, whack, 'cop that', swish, thunk, 'gotcha, you bastard'.

When daylight broke, the camp resembled a battleground. Tom, bleary eyed but happy, gave us the score: Burrows, 125; the rats, nil.

Tommy Burrows and mates in Camooweal, 1960. Left to Right: Alan Simpson, Tommy Burrows, Ernie McCarthy and Noel Willetts. Photo: the author

In more recent years Tom lived at Alice Springs, where he had his own small residence at Ted Egan's 'Sinkatinny Downs'. When Ted was away, Tom acted as caretaker, but always had a few irons in the fire himself. At one time he bred and sold poultry. These he kept in a very large fenced area behind his house. His method of doing business was simple: he took the money and let the buyer run down the purchased birds himself. I sometimes visited Tom, and one of my most vivid memories is of a portly cafe proprietor vainly pursuing a fleet-footed turkey, while Tom drank a beer and shouted encouragement.

Tom also had an early morning rubbish contract. In his small red truck, he went around the Alice Springs business houses picking up cartons and other dry rubbish. He got going before the shops opened and the traffic started. This was just as well, for Tom tended to rewrite the traffic code as he went. He knew just about everyone, and his cheerful shouted greetings to the early risers used to echo down the almost empty streets. I have travelled with Tom on these runs; it is an experience I will never forget.

Thomas Anzac Burrows died on 15 February 1999. He was a great Australian whose life story is undeniable proof of the supremacy of the human spirit over adversity.

The Burrows Morning Run

The tourists come to Alice Springs, they come from near and far,
Some travellers come in aeroplanes, and some by motor car.
There's some who like to ride the rails and catch the famous Ghan,
Some hitch a ride and get there by whatever means they can.
They come to Alice Springs because there's much to see and do,
Some take a trip to Simpson's Gap and some climb Uluru.

They travel out to Alice Springs from many climes and lands
To see the famous masters games or Henley on the sands.
A lot buy prints and artefacts to take back overseas,
And if they don't find value here, they're pretty hard to please.
Some tourists like historic sites and photograph the 'spring',
But most prefer to have a beer and hear Ted Egan sing.

The tourists come to Alice Springs, they come by day and night,
The pious and the pagan, and the sober and the tight.
Of all the sights that they will see, when all is said and done,
There's none can hold a candle to the Burrows morning run.
And fortunate indeed are they, those travellers who have been
Beside a living legend in his famous red machine.

The Dachshund-Pony Cross

Just twelve months ago tomorrow, I recall the fact with sorrow,
I signed the pledge teetotal and renounced all alcohol.
No greater soak existed till the 'Salvos' got me listed,
But the tale of my salvation is, I fear, a trifle droll.
I had come in with a drover all the way from 'Sanded Over',
For two weary months of boredom we had sweated day and night,
And our skins were fairly cracking from the moisture content lacking
When we struck a Western township by the name of Sandy-blight.

Now our cheques were nice and healthy, we were feeling rather wealthy,
So we started on a bender that extended for a week.
Oh! we made the grog look silly, for we drank it from a billy,
And I ended in the horrors at our camp upon the creek.
In the DTs I was running brumby mobs whose native cunning
Wasn't equalled by the rodents of a well-known public place,
For their speed was hackle raising, their sagacity amazing
As we crossed the creeks and ridges at a denny-hazer pace.

For six days and nights I chased 'em, though I never once outpaced 'em
And the West lay far behind us as the farmlands came in view.
Over fence and field I followed, past the sties where porkers wallowed,
For I swore that I would wheel 'em if they went to Timbuktu.
Then the nag that I was riding seemed to shorten in his striding
As we passed a cocky's farmlet in a belt of gooseberry trees,
And for that I soon accounted, for I found when I dismounted
That his legs from ceaseless riding were all worn off to the knees.

Well, that rang the final curtain on the brumby hunt for certain,
But in my drunken nightmare I conceived a grand idea.
I could see my wallet swelling as I sought the cocky's dwelling
With my erstwhile brumby runner pussy-footing in the rear.
Now the farmer bloke seemed chary when I met him in the dairy,
But I raised my old Akubra and politely called him 'boss'.
Oh! my luck was never better, for my plan worked to the letter
And I sold my stumpy charger as a dachshund-pony cross.

But when the daylight found me with the dead marines around me
I swore with deadly fervour that I'd never drink again,
While my cobbers thought me balmy, that same day I joined the 'army'
For worse times or for better, I signed up with shaking pen.
Though I sometimes get to thinking that I'd like a bout of drinking,
I can't regard its absence from my lifestyle as a loss,
For my spirits still are daunted and nocturnally I'm haunted
By the sawn-off apparition of the dachshund-pony cross.

The Riding of the Debil

(As told by Murranji Mick. With apologies to the late Will Ogilvie.)

Now, you youngsters think you're riders when you break a colt or two,
Why you wouldn't make offsiders for the breakers that I knew;
I have listened to your blowin' and the flamin' blatherskite
Of your ridin' and your throwin' every flamin' day and night.
Your tongues are always waggin' of some harmless flamin' moke,
But you never hear me braggin' of the outlaws that I broke.

I was never one for glory, as I've often said before,
But I'll tell a dinkum story if you'll hold your flamin' jaw.
It was some time in November, and the year was thirty-four,
I was breakin', I remember, on a run called Bullgalore;
That was in the Never Never near the town of Shantyview
On the Bullmakanka River where the crockagaters chew.

Well, one day we heard a rumour from the mailman passing through,
And although it was a boomer he was certain it was true,
For it seemed old Jock McGrilly up at Grabagrogangrin
Had a flamin' outlaw filly that he wanted broken in.
She would buck and kick and trample and she'd killed a dozen men,
Oh! she was a fair example of the nags we handled then.

Yes, she was a real humdinger and McGrilly said he'd pay
A tenner to the ringer who could tame her in a day.
Well, those days I liked to gamble so I ran me horses in
And I started at an amble up to Grabagrogangrin.
I unpacked and boiled me billy where I camped beside the yard,
And I saw the outlaw filly a sorta lookin' at me hard.

Now the Debil they had named her and the ringers in the huts
Said the flamin' man who tamed her would be needin' tons of guts.
All her victims had been recent but no man could ever say
That they didn't do things decent up the Bullmakanka way;
For they made a cemetery where they laid 'em nice and neat,
At their heads a conkaberry and the goat yard at their feet.

Jimmy Bunion came to ride her, he had just come off a spree,
But he said that once astride her he would be a sight to see.
Though his skill was quite outstandin', he was buried in an hour,
For he broke his neck in landin' on the flamin' windmill tower.
Dunno why they buried Bunion, he'd have kept till Kingdom come
He was pickled like an onion from his bouts on shanty rum.

Then along came Billy Gundy, of Gulf riders he was best,
But they laid him one black Monday by the goat yard with the rest.
Next a ringer called Moskeeta from the Booraloola side
Rode three hundred miles to beat her, and they said that he could ride.
With his big toe in the stirrup and a six or eight inch grin
He could stick like golden syrup to a hungry piccanin.

In a high unnervin' treble he'd corroboree as he swayed,
But his swan song on the Debil never made the hit parade.
Well, I had a reputation and I thought about the cash,
So I told them at the station that I'd like to have a lash.
It was early when I caught her as the dawn began to break,
I was windy of her sorta, but I reckoned I'd be jake.

It was just light when I mounted, but the sun shone in me eye
On the third buck that I counted, for she rooted pretty high.
Talk about acceleration, like a bullet from a gun
She departed from the station and lit out across the run.
She was buckin' hell-for-leather and the gibbers flew like chaff
When we left the ground together and she cut a cloud in half.

We had reached the flamin' river with me senses pretty blurred
When I felt the Debil quiver but she took it like a bird,
And there was a mile of clearance 'bove the coolibahs, I swear,
From the pigmy-like appearance of a swaggie fishin' there.
Well, I rode her like a hero till we came to Shantyview
And I waved me old sombrero to some fellers that I knew.

Then the Debil gave a nicker and she cartwheeled off one hoof
And she threw me in a flicker through the flamin' lock-up roof.
Then the sergeant, to me sorrow, came and said, 'How are you mate,
You'll appear some time tomorrow up before our magistrate.'
Well, you should have seen the guiver when I fronted up next day,
To be fined a flamin' fiver or a week in Fannie Bay.

Now the magistrate was rugged in a boozy Top End way,
And I knew me case was buggered, still I thought I'd have me say,
Oh! I knew I was a goner, I was handcuffed to the sarge,
But I said look here, your honour, what the flamin' hell's the charge?
Well, his voice rose to a bellow, 'Don't bung on you didn't know,
We aint found your plane yet, fellow, but the charge was flyin' low.'

Brumby George in the City

I'm down in this here town at last and hell, writes Brumby George,
The flaming people swarm like ants, the streets are like a gorge.
It's sorta opened up me eyes, but I can tell you mate
I aim to hold me own down here although I've started late.
I know that I'm behind the times and been up North too long
And if a feller called me slow I wouldn't call him wrong.
But I am settling in down here and learning city ways,
And I can see the wicked waste of all me younger days.

I ain't the mug some fellers think and I ain't bought no shares
In statues or in swimming pools or city parks and squares.
The traffic, though, I reckon mate has sorta got me beat
I'd rather face a scrubber bull than cross the flaming street.
The city blokes all go like hell as though they're running late
So they've got lights on corners here to draft the bludgers mate,
These lights will block the flaming lead and string the city push
They work the cars and trucks down here like cattle in the bush.

These city blokes fly for the grog like bullocks round a float,
One night I wanders in a pub to pour one down me throat,
I elbows in to get a rum and just gets to the trough
When some big jackaroo sings out: 'I'm sorry gents it's off.'
'Ho! is it off?' I says to him, 'you ruddy rouseabout
Just fill them glasses round the bar for this is Brumby's shout.'
He stands and looks at me awhile, agaping like a cod,
And then he grabs the flaming phone and rings the vicious squad.

I'd heard about this vicious squad, they're pretty tough to meet,
And so I downs the barman bloke and hits out up the street.
By crikey mate the pubs is flash, there's carpet here like grass,
They've even got a water spout to clean your flaming arse.
The tucker here's a bushie's dream all wrote out on a list,
First day I strolls in sober like, me quart pot in me fist.
I looks around to find a chair and has no luck at all,
And so I squats down on me heels, me back agin the wall.

I dunno what I done or said to cause a flaming stir,
A little waitress ambles up and says, 'Excuse me Sir.'
I ain't no sir I says to her, me name is Brumby Jones
Just boil me quart and make it strong and grill a few rib bones.
But they have got me broken now to eat like humans ought,
One waitress here has worked out West, she ain't a bad old sort.
I took her out the other night, I tell you it was grand
The way she sorta looked at me and held me flaming hand.

Me name ain't Brumby Jones no more, reluctantly I owns,
I sorta like the idea now of being Mr Jones.
Me flaming eyes is opened like and I can tell you mate
I'll mix it with this city push although I've started late.
I'm settling in down here I am and learning city ways,
And I can see the wicked waste of all me younger days.
I dunno when I'm shooting through, but it's a certain bet
That I'll be back at Grasstree by the finish of the wet.
I'll be there when the muster starts up far off Rocky gorge
But until then I'll live it up, your old mate Brumby George.

Brisbane or the Bush

I spent most of my working life in the bush. Twice I took on jobs in the city for a time, but the bush always called me back. On the first of these sojourns in the big smoke I ended up working at a meatworks. Having decided to get a job in Brisbane, I soon realised I had little or no idea of how to go about achieving my ambition. My credentials, first rate in the bush, were of no value whatever in the city. I made a few inquiries, called on some business houses and got nowhere at all. I was feeling pretty browned off and ready to give the idea away when I got a lucky break.

I was staying at the Shandon private hotel in upper Edward Street at the time; I usually stayed there when on holidays in Brisbane. The Shandon was owned and run by a Mrs Hall, a grand old lady who took a motherly interest in her guests and of course knew everyone's business. The good lady was aware of my plight and decided to have a heart to heart talk to me over the breakfast table one morning.

She listened to my story of rejection, then said, 'Young man, why don't you try working behind the counter in a shop. You don't need special training for that?'

The idea was anathema to me, and I said no. The resident taxi driver, who was also at the table, spread butter liberally on a piece of toast and, avoiding Mrs Hall's critical look, put in his two bob's worth. 'Why don't you try the meatworks?'

I brightened up at once. Working at a meatworks appealed to me straight away; I'd be around cattle again, even if most of them were carcasses. My spirits, however, were soon dashed.

'Of course,' said the resident taxi driver, 'you would have to join the union. The Australian Meat Industry Employees Union controls the workforce and I believe it's almost a closed shop.'

I had nothing against unions. I'd always been a member of the AWU, although in all my time in stockcamps I'd only seen one organiser visit the ringers. I thanked the taxi driver and decided to follow up the meatworks idea. Next day I found out that the AMIEU had its offices in the Trades Hall, not far down Edwards Street from the Shandon. I located the office without trouble and walked in. A heavily built man behind a desk looked me over.

'Are you a union member?'

'No, but I'd like to join.'

'Would you? So would a lot of people. Have you had any experience in the industry?'

I told him I could slaughter a beast. I didn't say that I'd done the job in the bush and on the ground rather than on a gallows. I also thought it unnecessary to inform him that the beast had often belonged to someone else.

The man behind the desk thought for a moment. 'Do you know anyone in the union?'

I shook my head, and that seemed to please him. 'Well, you'll have to be nominated and seconded by two union members who know you. Here's the forms.'

As I left the union office I had the distinct impression the man behind the desk did not expect to see me again. It was obvious to me that the AMIEU was not at that time conducting a membership drive. Nevertheless, I was happy. I had cleared the first hurdle. All I had to do now was to find two union members who would provide me with an entree to the union. Although my funds were perilously low, I walked on down to Queen Street, strolled into the Australian Hotel and celebrated with a couple of beers.

As the Shandon was a bed and breakfast establishment, I did not see my advisers until the next morning. At breakfast I told them of my progress and asked their advice on where to find union members. Mrs Hall thought I should try butcher's shops, but the resident taxi driver gave her a pitying look and, reaching for the marmalade, spoke with conviction. 'No, I'll tell you where to go. Slip out to the Cannon Hill saleyards. The place is full of broken down stockmen; they'll fix you up.'

I thanked him and realised the truth of the old saying, 'If you want to know anything ask a taxi driver.' I finished breakfast and set out for Cannon Hill. By luck I arrived as the men were starting their smoko break. I spotted a wiry character squatting on his heels against a yard post. It is a position favoured by stockmen who have to make do without chairs. He looked every inch a horseman, so I strolled over, introduced myself and found I was talking to Colin Bell, an outstanding horseman of his day. We yarned for a while and shortly after he organised the two signatures I needed. I drew a blank when I approached the office about a job there, but left in high spirits. Another obstacle had been overcome.

When I returned to the city, I called into the union office and handed in the application papers. I also paid my union dues. The man behind the desk, looking somewhat surprised, asked, 'Do these men know you?'

I nodded. 'Yes, like me they're from the bush.' It wasn't really a lie, they did know me, if only for a few hours.

'What happens now?' I asked the man behind the desk.

'Well, there will be a union meeting on Monday night at eight. A vote will be taken then to decide if we are going to accept any new members.'

I had to be satisfied with that. I walked up to the Shandon. It was Friday and the prospect of a Brisbane weekend without adequate funds was never rosy; however, I would have to amuse myself as best I could. I spent some time on a verse I was writing, lazed around in the Botanical Gardens and listened to the Salvation Army band on Sunday night in lower Edward Street.

Finally Monday night came and I went down to the Trades Hall and found the room where the meeting was being held. I noticed two chaps sitting outside the room, but went in and sat down inside. After a fair amount of general business the time came to vote on the fate of the aspiring members. The names of the two other applicants and myself were read out, together with the details on the tendered forms. When the vote was taken, my hand was amongst the first to go up. The decision was made—I was in. After the meeting the union officials called the two men in from outside. As I was already in, I waited in the aisle to join them.

It was then that the man from behind the desk spotted me. He glared balefully at me.

'Have you been in the meeting?' he hissed.

'Yes, you told me there was to be a meeting tonight.'

'A meeting for bloody members,' he replied in a hoarse undertone. 'You were supposed to wait outside. Your presence could have made the whole proceedings unconstitutional.'

There is something ridiculous about a man delivering a diatribe sotto voce. I suppressed the urge to laugh and apologised with as much grace as I could muster. I had, after all, been in the wrong place at the wrong time.

Somewhat mollified by my contrite manner, the man from behind the desk proceeded to enlighten us on the benefits of unionism and in particular on what the AMIEU would do for us. We were told the union would get us jobs. All we had to do was to wait in the car park each morning; at seven o'clock the union officials would select men for the day's vacancies.

I went back to the Shandon satisfied with the night's work. There was now only one hurdle left—getting a job, and the union, it seemed, would provide me with that.

At six next morning I jogged down to the Trades Hall to find some 30 hopefuls queued up there before me. Within the next half hour there were as many more behind me. A little after seven a union official arrived and selected 10 men from the first dozen or so. The rest of us were advised to go home and try again on the morrow. Wednesday and Thursday mornings were much the same, although I had managed to get near the front both times. I began to depair of ever getting a job.

Back at the Shandon, I was gloomily breakfasting on tea and toast when the resident taxi driver walked in. 'Have you seen today's paper?' he asked.

I shook my head. 'Why, has war been declared?'

'No, but there's a job there for you.' He tossed over the paper.

Sure enough, there it was. An advertisement for a stockman at Borthwick's meatworks. You bloody beaut! But had it been filled? I almost ran to the phone, rang the number given and asked for the manager. After what seemed like an eternity he came on the line. He asked me what experience I'd had with cattle and checked that I was a union member. The vacancy, he told me, had not been filled but was not of a permanent nature. I could start on Monday morning at eight if I wanted the job. Did I want the job! My bloody oath I did. I told the manager I'd be there Monday morning and hung up the phone. I went back to the breakfast table, shook the taxi driver's hand and told him taxi drivers should be running the country. He agreed and said I could buy him a ticket in the golden casket.

Later that day I thought it would be a courtesy to advise the union of my success. At the Trades Hall I strolled into the office and told the man behind the desk of my good fortune. He stood up and for a second I thought he was going to have a stroke.

'The union gets jobs for its members,' he stormed. 'You're not allowed to look for work outside the union.'

I'd had a gutful of the man behind the desk. For the first time, I believed I had the whip hand. Resisting the temptation to call him an arrogant bastard, I spoke slowly and clearly. 'Shut up for a moment and listen to me. I'm no scab; this job was advertised for union members only. I'm a member of your damn union, I've got the job and I'm bloody well going to keep it.'

I turned and walked out of the office, leaving him standing open mouthed behind his desk. I thought my actions may perhaps have precipitated an industrial dispute; however, on Monday morning when I arrived at Borthwicks I was relieved to find no sign of a picket line. The yard boss showed me what my duties were. All I had to do was to keep the cattle moving up the elevated race to the killing pen. Some sensitive souls may have found the job distasteful, but as far as I was concerned bullocks were bred to be slaughtered, and I had a job again with cattle. The bloke I had replaced was off with a broken leg. My job would last until he returned to work. For the next three weeks I enjoyed myself immensely. The work was easy and it was great to be in the company of stockmen again.

When the injured man returned to work, the management decided rather than let me go they would use me as a spare man. If anyone was away from any one of the many gangs, I would stand in for them. I found myself on hides one day, hooves the next and horns the day after. A week after leaving the stockwork, I was given a week on the digesters. This was where the bones, stripped of meat in the boning room below, were ground up for bonemeal. When I started there the foreman showed me the ropes. The bones came up from the boning room in hoppers. My job was to throw the bones down the digester shute then press a button that returned the empty hopper while bringing up another full one. It seemed a rather simple job to me. When the foreman had departed, a chap from the boning room came to see me. I had noticed two large steel cabinets standing by the wall, and the man from the boning room put me in the picture. Occasionally, he told me, a cut of meat may come up with the bones. Would I mind putting it in one of the cabinets?

I thought for a moment, then agreed. The management knew the cabinets were there, and they seemed to have no other function.

The job was rather boring. The only distraction was the steady stream of fillets and rumps that came up with the bones. By the end of the shift, both cabinets were chock-a-block. I had trouble shutting the doors. As the whistle blew at four o'clock, up came the boners. The cabinets were flung open, and in less time than it takes to tell, the meat was stowed away in lunch bags. Meat workers who came to work swinging those bags went home weighed down by them. They walked as though suffering from some strange and sporadic spine affliction. Now and again I carried a prime rump steak home to the admirable Mrs Hall.

The money was good at the works, but living at the Shandon had its drawbacks. It only provided bed and breakfast and I found having to buy lunch and dinner expensive as well as a nuisance. It was also a long way from the New Farm ferry. So when a room-mate who worked in the Valley suggested we look for full board and lodging, I readily agreed, providing we found a place closer to the ferry.

I left it in his hands and on the following weekend he gave me the good news that he had found a place at a very reasonable figure. As he had only spoken to the lady on the phone, we both hopped on a tram to look the place over. It was quite close to the ferry, we found, and looked OK from the street. On our ringing the doorbell, a large formidable female appeared and advised us in no uncertain terms that she believed that door-to-door salesmen should go to blazes. As she was about to slam the door in our faces, I managed to tell her we were there about the room.

'Well, why didn't you say so,' she snapped, 'instead of standing there wasting my time. Come in, then, but I can tell you right now I won't stand for no boozing or hanky-panky in this house.'

We looked at one another, then shrugged and followed her into the dwelling. The room she showed us was quite comfortable and roomy, so when we were alone we talked it over and decided that despite our landlady's sour nature we would move in. We were told two sisters had rented the room before us. One thing that struck me was the large notices she had stuck up behind the bedroom door, in the hall, and just about everywhere else. They warned guests not to do this, and told them that they must do that, all couched in very direct terms. We were given a guided tour of the bathroom, with our landlady verbally reinforcing the messages printed on the signs adorning the walls. By the bath stood a sinister-looking gas heater. Its welfare, we were told, was of great importance. I took it for granted that anyone unlucky enough to misuse the thing would bring her wrath down upon his head.

My mate and I caught a tram back to the city, said our goodbyes to Mrs Hall and enlisted the help of the resident taxi driver to move us into our new lodgings. To bring a bit of masculinity to the room, I dug my whip and spurs out and hung them up on the curtain rods, an act for which I was later to be severely chastised. When the dinner bell went that night, we went into the dining room to find that there were two other guests in the establishment.

One was a rather anaemic girl who was extremely timid. She never lifted her face from her plate during the meal, and when finished she scuttled off like a startled rabbit. The other guest was something else entirely. He could have been 70 or more, a grizzled veteran of life's hard knocks. He looked as though he had seen better days, but the shaggy brows could not hide the gleam in his eyes. I decided there was life in the old dog yet. After the meal, our landlady sat back and spoke.

'I like to know something about my guests.' She fixed her unblinking gaze on me. 'Now, young man, just what do you do for a living?'

'Well,' I said, 'I'm a bushman, but at the moment I'm working at a meatworks.'

'Great,' said the grizzled veteran, 'then perhaps you can bring home some decent meat for a change.'

To my surprise, the lady ignored him and turned her attention to the salesman from the Valley. Apart from having him as a room-mate at the Shandon, I knew very little about him myself. He was a solid individual of medium height with closely cropped hair and a ginger moustache. He tended to surround himself with what I believed was carefully feigned mystery. I sat back and waited.

In reply to her question the salesman gave a cheeky grin and said, 'Oh! I sell things.'

'Do you?' our landlady said. 'What sort of things?'

'Oh! This and that, bits and pieces, one thing and another.'

Our hostess was not impressed. 'Not a very suitable career, I'm afraid. A man should have a trade. My late husband, God rest him, had a trade until he fell under the influence of the demon drink.'

'What trade did he follow?' I asked innocently.

Before she could reply, the grizzled veteran spoke. 'My sister,' he said, establishing his position in the menage. 'Is a bit sensitive about that. George was a farrier, and a good one. He worked for a brewery and could shoe a draughthorse while some blokes were thinking about it. But the drink got him. Employing George at a brewery was like putting a cannibal in charge of a creche. At the end I reckon George would drink the piss from a brewer's horse.'

The landlady rose to her feet. 'Bill, I will not have you talk like that. Please leave the table.'

We left and followed Bill out of the room. We passed him chuckling to himself in the hall. I suspected that he had been subjected to petticoat discipline for years and finding himself with a male audience had gone to his head a bit. He certainly took the opportunity to get a bit of his own back.

On the following Monday I was put in the freezers for the week. We were in for 30 minutes then relieved for the same length of time, to allow us to thaw out. I didn't mind the job, but was happy, the following week, to join the gall gang. I found this rather interesting. The gall was collected from the gall bladder of the animals killed and put into huge vats. Large paddles kept the gall moving while the heated vats gradually reduced it to a treacle-like consistency. Finally the gall was put into 44 gallon (200 litre) drums and sold—overseas, I believe. There is not a lot of a beast that is wasted, believe me. The blokes used to say that the only thing they missed was the bullock's bellow.

With money to spare, I was now enjoying myself in the city. I went to the races each Saturday and was a regular at the fights at the old Brisbane stadium. The main attraction at the races was the horses. I had never been a gambler and my habit of having the occasional bet had been dampened when I had had a punt on the Caulfield Cup the previous year.

A few of us were in Camooweal for a few days, and were enjoying ourselves in the bar on the Saturday when the local SP bookie arrived. Without knowing the horses, I had a quid on Royal Gem to win. He entered the wager in a tattered notebook, but did not give me a ticket. I promptly forgot about the bet, and it was not until that night that I realised I had backed the winner.

I ran the bookie to earth and asked for my money. He looked at me blankly and told me the bet on Royal Gem had been collected by a fencer. I found it useless to argue with him. In the end he told me that if I wanted my winnings I would have to see the fencer.

I managed to retrieve the money, then returned to the bar, where I shouted for my mates. Backing horses, I told them, was a mug's game. They told me they knew how I felt, as it was written all over my face.

After another two weeks relieving on various gangs, I was put in charge of the lard room. Not a big promotion, as it was a one man job, although I was promised an offsider. It was then that disaster struck at our lodgings. The gas heater in the bathroom had been playing up for some time. The pilot light went out at times and I refused to use the damned contraption. As a cool spell had hit Brisbane, the salesman from the Valley decided to take a hot bath. I walked past the bathroom as he was endeavouring, stark naked, to light the brute of a thing.

'This bloody thing won't go,' he complained.

I explained he would have to use a match and gave him a box of mine. What I hadn't realised was that he still had the gas going.

I hadn't gone five paces when a thunderous explosion shook the building. I raced back to find the bathroom door off its hinges and my room-mate standing with his body hair singed, and covered in black soot. The gas heater was on the floor still aflame and looking for all the world like a scaled-down version of a plane crash.

I turned the gas and water taps off just as our landlady burst into the room.

'What have you done?' she screeched.

'I've done nothing,' my scorched room-mate cried, reaching for a towel. 'But this thing has nearly DONE for me.'

'I'll sue you,' the virago roared. 'I'll sue for damages.'

At that the salesman fell to the floor.

'Quick, phone the ambulance. This man could be badly hurt,' I told her.

As she left I walked over to the salesman. He looked up at me and winked. 'How was that for a dive?'

'Bloody feeble,' I told him, 'you broke your fall with your hands.'

Things finally settled down. My room-mate's injuries were superficial, and within a week a new electric water heater had been installed in the bathroom. Life at the boarding house returned to what could loosely be termed as normal.

I enjoyed my new job in the lard room. The lard or dripping came up to me as solid blocks weighing 56 pounds (25 kilograms). A wire frame was used to cut the lard into rough pats, which were weighed to one pound (450 grams) and finally wrapped. The pats were never cut accurately, and lard had to be either added or removed. To help me in this arduous activity, the powers that be gave me an offsider as promised. I often wished they hadn't, for he was a gangling youth and the most uncoordinated individual I have ever known. His clumsiness had to be seen to be believed. I thought he must improve, but he never did. Finally I did my block and called him a hopeless bloody malingerer who was as useless as tits on a boar pig. He didn't take umbrage at my abuse, nor did he improve.

On Saturday, as was my custom, I went to the fights. A five round preliminary bout was announced and, to my amazement, my clumsy off-sider climbed through the ropes and sat down in the blue corner. Opposite him in the red corner sat a rough character who looked strong enough to hold a bull out to piddle. I sat back and waited for the carnage to start, and start it did, as soon as the bell went. My bumbling offsider slipped out of his corner and proceeded to belt the stuffing out of the neanderthal type from the red corner. Pat Hill, the referee, stopped the fight in the second round. After the fights I made my way thoughtfully home, vowing to be a little more circumspect when addressing my off-sider in future.

I had been working in the lard room for about a month when the chap I had relieved returned from holidays. I was back relieving on the various yard gangs for a few weeks, when one Saturday morning I met a couple of ringers I knew in the Australian Hotel. We had a few beers and talked generally for a while, then one of them asked how long I'd been on holiday. I explained I was living and working in Brisbane.

He looked at me in disbelief. 'Working down here! You must be bloody mad. There's grass girth high out back.'

'It's been a good season then,' I said.

'Good season! There's clover on the Cooper, they say.'

Clover on the Cooper, I thought, clover on the bloody Cooper. That did it. On Monday morning I gave notice at Borthwicks. The call of the bush could not be denied.

The Bushman from the Burke

The rugged bushman rolled his swag, he'd come from off the Burke,
He knew the sprawling stations there would soon be starting work.
He'd had his fill of city life, the time had come to go,
He caught a cab to Roma Street, a station bushmen know.
He threw his swag upon the train and found himself a seat
Beside a girl with golden hair and features pure and sweet.
She gave our friend a timid smile, a greeting tinged with fear,
The bushman said some words to her that no one else could hear.

In startled fright the lass sprang up, hell bent upon escape
And 'Rape,' she screamed out as she ran, 'Help me! attempted rape!'
The bushman looked in shocked surprise. 'Hey, what's your little game?'
Then from the platform just outside a charging policeman came.
He grabbed the bushman by the arm. 'Right, what have you to say?
That girl just said you threatened rape, that's why she ran away.'
'I told her where I'm going to, I swear that's all I said
And then she flamin' ups and goes right off her flamin' head.'

'I know your type,' the policeman said. 'A deviate and pest
It plainly is my duty now to make a quick arrest.'
'It seems to me,' the bushman growled, 'you won't let me explain
And I will do you grievous harm if I don't catch this train.'
He took the cursing bushman to the station master's den,
A jaded sergeant came and asked, 'What are the charges then?'
'Attempted rape,' the policeman crowed. 'The evidence is clear,
He tried to rape a passenger, she's traumatised with fear.'

'You've set me up,' the bushman cried, 'but I have read about
You city push that prey upon us blokes from further out,
I never tried to rape no one, it's like I said before
I told her where I'm going to, just that and nothing more,
I tried to be real friendly like, I even raised me hat
And told her where I'm going to, there ain't no crime in that.'
'Hang on! Hang on!' the sergeant said. 'Why did she run in fright?
How could the place you're going to cause panic-stricken flight?

'I cannot see from what you say just why the woman fled
So tell me slowly word for word precisely WHAT you said.'
'Well, I said I'm goin' to Bullya and then she goes berserk,
Youse musta heard of Bullya town, old Bullya on the Burke,
I wish I'd stayed in Bullya now and dodged the likes of youse
And had me spree at Bullya pub and shopped at Donahues.'
The weary sergeant groaned aloud. 'You still can catch that train
So go to flaming Boulia, Sir, and don't come back again.'

Ringer's Farewell

The city now seems dull and stale—
The lights have lost their lustre,
We miss the bush mates rough and hale—
The branding and the muster.
We've had our fun with reckless glee,
Cards, women, wine and singing,
It's high time now to end the spree
And once more go back ringing.

With blasé smile we've done it grand,
Gone paddock at the races,
Made merry in the way we'd planned
In dives and other places.
But when from bar to outback plain
Nostalgia takes us winging,
It's time to roll the swag again
And once more go back ringing.

We've dined in state and tête-à-tête,
Of parties had our ration,
It seems a century since we ate
In careless stockcamp fashion.
For further out we've shown the flag
And set a few hearts singing,
It's high time now to roll the swag
And once more go back ringing.

It's raining now through neon glare,
Though lawns could not be greener,
We wonder if they've had their share
Out on the far Georgina.
A good west wind came with the rain
A hint of gidgee bringing.
It's time to catch the outback train
And once more go back ringing.

Wild Men and Windlasses

Brennen reined in his horse on the side of the ridge and, with eyes narrowed, surveyed the landscape beyond. His lead packhorse drew up beside him, rubbing his head on Brennen's leg to gain relief from the bush flies. The rider pushed him away with a curse and checked that the saddle bag hanging from his saddle dees was still there. Brennen grunted with relief; in that saddle were gems, the result of a month of solitary hard work. Brennen was a loner. The location of his opal mine was known to none but this secretive, and often unsociable, hermit from the hills south-west of Kynuna, and he took great care that his mine should never be found. He never camped close to where he was working and shifted camp regularly, choosing a different route to the mine each time so that no one would be able to follow his tracks.

Brennen had a thinly disguised contempt for the opal gougers who worked the Kynuna field south of where he mined the precious gems. Most of them were on government money, an idea that was anathema to him.

An opal buyer who paid regular visits to Kynuna was due on the mail on the morrow. He knew Brennen's opal and the loner was confident of getting a fair deal. The only time Brennan was ever seen in Kynuna was when the buyer was in town. Brennen was a man who aroused a lot of curiosity, a taciturn character with a secret mine that produced the finest quality opal.

Brennen knocked the ashes from his pipe on a kneepad. He spat, then checked the time by the sun. There were cattle pads running in to water at the end of the ridge. He would ride down those pads shortly, and cattle walking out to feed would wipe out his tracks. Later he would take a roundabout route into Kynuna. No one was going to backtrack Brennen to his mine. He would camp down on the bank of the Diamantina that night. But he would not sleep. Men had been murdered for less than he had in that saddlebag. He would douse his fire and sit awake cradling a Winchester rifle until daylight.

Brennen sold his opal next day, after haggling for some time with the buyer. Not altogether satisfied with the deal, he made his way to the post office and banked the notes. Then he headed for the pub to have a few drinks. He had time to spare, for he would not start back before dark. Brennen drank alone, making it plain he wanted no company. There was a group of noisy shearers in the bar, and one of their number was drinking next to him. Somehow or other a sixpence fell to the floor between them. Both men claimed it and a brawl started. Brennen went down, striking his head a sickening blow. The injury proved fatal. Brennen, the man with the richest claim in the whole area, died fighting over a sixpenny piece.

After his death, interest continued to grow in Brennen's opal mine. It had to be out there somewhere, and many attempts were made to locate it. The dead man had covered his tracks well, however. Good prospectors, like Mick Cheadle and my brother Jeff, spent weeks combing the area without success. They did find another mine that had been lost for many years, one that had been worked by a chap named Peter Karfe, but Brennen's mine remains lost in the rough country south-west of Kynuna.

Opal is nature's greatest treasure. When found it needs no faceting: from a nick in its surface, its vivid colours blaze forth. Men who fall under its spell seldom, if ever, get over their love affair with the most beautiful of gems.

Opal was formed millions of years ago by water that leeched down through deposits of sedimentary sandstone to form hydro-silica—a mixture of water and silica. For many years the reason for opal's prismatic capability remained a mystery, until the electron microscope finally unmasked its secrets. Gem-quality opal is made up of neatly stacked plates cemented together by hydro-silica. This gives the stone the ability to break up white light like a rainbow. In potch, or common opal, these plates are not uniform and do not have the prismatic capacity of gem opal. In Queensland, opal is found in boulders and in sandstone that is close to an ironstone band.

Hard on the heels of the overlanders and settlers who opened up the outback were the packhorse prospectors. These hardy characters were interested only in what might be secreted deep beneath the inhospitable landscape of the interior. Despite having to rely on horses, they missed very little, as their modern counterparts can vouch for. Many a prospector in a four-wheel drive vehicle has arrived at what he thought was new ground, miles from water, to find evidence of the activities of the old-time packhorse brigade.

During the 1970s most of the prospecting and mining was done in the pre-Cambrian landforms around Cloncurry, an area rich in copper and other minerals. The country further south, being non-metalliferous, was far less promising, and had been inundated over millions of years by the long dry inland sea. Covering most of inland Australia, it is what geologists call desert sandstone country. Its topography is mixed, being made up of creek and river flats together with low ridges and rough, flat-topped hills. The sedimentary deposits of this area were laid down during the Cretaceous era, and hidden deep in its sandstone layers are opals.

The first gem-quality opal found in Queensland was in 1883 at Bull Creek, west of Quilpie in the far west of the state. Two years later opal was found at the Alladin mine, north-west of Eromanga, and a company was formed to market the gems, which it did with some success. In 1887 a tough bushman named Cragg arrived at the Mayne River, a tributary of the Diamantina, and started prospecting. It is not known if Cragg had worked on the opal fields to the south, but he appeared to know what he was looking for. He found opal and his mine became known simply as Cragg's mine.

The country up along the Mayne is very rugged indeed. In the late 1950s I drove a mob of Territory bullocks up the Mayne and over the range at its headwaters. There was next to no grass and, as a cattleman, I decided that the Mayne River area was next to worthless. When I was taking the plant back after delivering the mob, I spent a little time with the Martyr family at Mayneside Station. On talking with Mrs Martyr, I realised the place was steeped in history.

By 1888 Cragg was producing good quality opal and interest in the area grew. He was camped on a waterhole below the junction of Horse Creek and Hyde Park Creek; these two join to form the Mayne River. The waterhole was close to Mayneside Station, and became the camping ground for newly arrived opal gougers. These men began prospecting up the tributaries of the Mayne, including New Year Creek. Soon other mines were producing opal, including Carlisles and the Poison claim.

At this time the outback was enjoying a period of rapid growth. Stations were being taken up and townships were being developed, with wagons and coaches raising the dust on newly made roads that linked the runs and embryo settlements of the far west. By 1880 the police had a strong presence in the Winton and Boulia districts. Winton boasted a sergeant and two constables, while Sub-Inspector Eglington was stationed at Boulia with a squad of native police. There were also native police at

Mrs Martyr Snr in front of the old store at Mayneside. Photo: Peter Knowls

Tulma barracks on the Diamantina River. By 1883 Winton had a greatly enlarged police force, a magistrate and a courthouse, where district court sittings were held.

The Goa tribe of Winton and the Pitta Pittas of Boulia, unlike their northern neighbours, the Kalkadoons, were regarded by the newcomers as more of a nuisance than a threat. Their presence was never a problem to the opal miners; however, in 1882 a part owner of Warnambool Station, a man named Young, was speared to death at the Old Station waterhole, and the Goas raided a wagon loaded with provisions en route to Warnambool. The Aborigines carried off a great deal of the supplies, including a consignment of kerosene soap. Knowing no better, they decided the soap must be tucker and hoed into it. A police party caught up with the culprits at Skull Hole, where they were 'dispersed'. When one considers the effect soap has on the digestive system, the unfortunate Aborigines would not have been hard to track.

The Goas were soon subdued and became fringe dwellers around stations and townships. The authorities hung brass plates around the neck of selected older Aborigines; these half moon shapes nominated the bearers as King so and so of such and such a tribe. It was an insult to their culture and a grotesque parody of English royalty.

The mining activity on the Mayne did not go unnoticed by commercial interests. A man named Pegler and his wife opened a store to cater for the needs of the miners, choosing a site close to the Mayneside Station homestead. Pegler, in his hastily erected building, was soon in business, but quickly won a reputation as a man who cheated the gougers, and came to be regarded by everyone as a poor type. One day when Pegler and his wife were away in Winton, a man whom the storekeeper had wronged arrived at the store. He gave Pegler's sister-in-law five minutes to get out, then set fire to the store and watched as it burnt to the ground.

In due course the police from Winton arrived to investigate the arson and began questioning the opal miners camped at the waterhole. One suspect was either frightened that an earlier sin would come to light, or was just sick of living, for after being questioned he returned to his claim and shot himself. This threw the police investigation into chaos. After dealing with the suicide and clearing the dead man of arson, they resumed questioning the opal gougers and finally arrested the culprit at his claim on New Year Creek.

All shafts put down in the early days of opal mining were put down by pick and shovel. These shafts were slightly rectangular in shape and many of them were quite deep. During the sinking, the overburden was brought to the surface with buckets and ropes attached to a windlass made from bush timber. The trunk of a small tree was usually employed as the barrel of the windlass; the barrel was supported on two forks, and a winding handle was attached to an iron bar driven into one end of it. Usually two men worked a claim: one down below loading the buckets, and the other on top, raising the dirt with the windlass. Roughly made ladders were also used in working shafts.

Mining development continued at the Mayne opal field, with new mines coming into production, including the Echo, Biddies and the White Cow. A new store was built close to the Mayneside homestead. It was constructed by a man named Lancashire, who had the mail run from Winton. The building had a bullock-hide floor and was later used as a storeroom by Jim Martyr and his family when they took over the station in 1925.

Present-day tourist area at Opalton. Photo: Peter Knowls

The most famous of all opal mines in the area of the Mayne was the Yellow Jimmy. According to the old timers, the Yellow Jimmy was a producer of beautiful gemstones. The claim was near Horse Creek, and was owned by two men who were still working it when World War I broke out. Both men went into Winton and enlisted in the AIF. They had thrown their picks and shovels down the shaft of the Yellow Jimmy, they said, and would return when the war was over. Whether or not the pair survived the war is not known, but they never returned to work the Yellow Jimmy.

Efforts were made by gougers to find the mine, which was rapidly gaining legendary qualities, but it was never found, and after World War I activities on the opal fields tapered off. In 1925, when Jim Martyr was on Mayneside, there were only a few old timers still working in the area.

During the period when the Mayne was producing opal, there was some prospecting done in other areas, but for the most part gougers concentrated on the established field on the headwaters of the Mayne River. There are reports, however, that a kangaroo shooter found opal near Mulga Creek; this area was later to become the famous Opalton field.

There was no mining done there until 1893 when McLennon pegged the Brilliant Claim. Other finds such as Conways Claim followed in quick succession, and the rush was on. By 1896 there was said to be between 500 and 600 men working claims in the area. The field produced a great deal of gem opal, the value of which can only be guessed at, for little was declared to the authorities. Private deals were seldom recorded, so government figures regarding opal production have always been suspect.

Water for the thriving community was brought from No Name Rock-hole and sold for 25 shillings for 100 gallons (455 litres). Good seasons meant there was plenty of grass for the growing number of miners' horses. The now booming town of Opalton soon had two hotels, a store, a police station and two butcher shops. Conway's butcher shop was a no frills affair, just a mulga tree for a gallows and a stump for a butcher's block. In the boom Conway slaughtered nine beasts a week. In 1894 a coach service was started from Longreach to Opalton. Winton now had a mining warden, and in an effort to attract business, a road was built from Warnambool to Opalton.

One of the first opal buyers in the field was a red-bearded character by the name of Clancy, who was in the employ of Wollaston, one of the best known and most influential opal dealers in Australia. Opal gougers are never happy about the price buyers offer for parcels of gemstones, which is mainly because gougers have an inflated idea of the value of their opal, and they ignore the fact that buyers do have to allow a margin for profit. The miners at Opalton made such a stir about prices that the government sent out H.L. Hyde, a valuer. Hyde found that Clancy was an honest man whose prices were fair. Other southern buyers on the field were Fairfax and Roberts, and a local buyer, John Hotton, was also active.

One of the greatest opal robberies of all time took place at Opalton. Two Germans sank a shaft down to 80 feet (25 metres), then abandoned it when they found no opal. Two gougers, Dick Shillington and a chap named Johnson, went down the shaft out of curiosity; on the way back up, they knocked off the end of a stone projecting from the wall of the shaft and discovered it was part of an opalised tree containing gem-quality opal. The pair broke up the huge stone after it was raised to the surface and the pieces are reported to have filled a wooden beer case. Castledine, the Opalton policeman, was away at Mayneside and had left the station keys with one of the publicans. That night the box of opal was locked in the jail for safekeeping.

Remains of the the baker's oven, Opalton. Photo: Peter Knowls

Next morning, to the consternation of the miners, the opal was missing. Its value in today's currency would be in the millions. The police from Winton were notified and arrived soon after to investigate the disappearance of the opal. They questioned the Opalton miners and the publican, and searched the camps, but did not elicit any useful information. The case was never solved, but for months after, miners searched old shafts, hollow logs and any other likely hiding spots in hope of finding the cache. All Shillington and Johnson got out of the find was the chips and small pieces of opal that were the result of breaking up the big stone.

The story of the Opalton robbery closely resembles one told by Ion Idriess in his book *Lightning Ridge*, but the location given by Idriess was Lightning Ridge. I have found it impossible to check the story, as records are non-existent. It is possible that Idriess, in writing his book, had heard about, and borrowed, the story.

I was first told the story of the robbery by Fred Holm at Winton in 1963. Fred was born at Windorah on 15 June 1880 and spent most of his

Fred Holm at the age of 92 in Winton. Photo: Brian Holm

life in the Winton district following horse breaking work and stockwork. Fred was over 80 when he talked with me, but his memory of the Opalton robbery was clear and concise. A fine horseman, Fred was quick to embrace motorised transport and in 1908 owned one of the first motorbikes in the area. He was very proud of the performance of his iron horse. Fred was always accurate when dealing with historical facts, but was not above spinning a yarn to his grandchildren.

Once, he told them, he rode his motorbike out to a station. When he got there he checked the oil and found it needed to be topped up. He asked the station's bookkeeper if any was available and was handed oil in an unlabelled bottle. He used about half and returned the bottle to the bookkeeper. On the way home he passed a drover with a pack of dogs; the dogs flew out and attacked the strange machine with gusto. When the melee was over, Fred found himself on the ground. Looking around for his bike, he was surprised to find it up a tree. Fred told the kids he had a lot of trouble getting the bike down out of that tree, but eventually, although puzzled by its behaviour, he continued on his trip. The next time he visited the station he asked the bookkeeper what sort of oil he had been given.

Fred Holm at Vindex Station, June 1907. Photo: Larry Holm

'Oh,' said the man, 'that was goanna oil.'

Fred Holm passed away on 21 May 1975, a few weeks short of his 96th birthday. His grave is in the Winton cemetery.

The Opalton field and Conways slumped in production at a time when opal prices were low, so the miners drifted away to new finds on Horse Creek. Trooper Castledine was transferred to the Duchess, the police barracks were purchased by George Cragg, and the hotels were removed and re-erected elsewhere. The last publican to leave was a man named Neal; he was later shot at Devoncourt Station near Cloncurry.

The Mayne fields continued to produce opal after Opalton's demise and a hotel was built at Mayne junction prior to the turn of the century. The site chosen was where the road from Mayneside met the Winton to Diamantina Lakes road near the junction of the two rivers. It had a rather chequered history, and the last licensee, a man named Edwards, is buried near the hotel. In the late 1940s the pub was pulled down and the material was used to help build the Munduran homestead.

Opal was found at the Kynuna field around the turn of the nineteenth century and a number of gougers were digging there before World War I. The opal was not far beneath the surface, but the quality and production

Headstone on grave of a young girl close to site of the old Mayne Junction Hotel. Photo: Peter Knowls

level was nowhere like that of Mayneside or Opalton. At one time the gougers were paid by the government to keep the field going.

Around the turn of the nineteenth century Charlie Rigby was employed as a dogger (dingo trapper) on Woodstock Station. The run was then owned by a man named Ellis, who also owned a small hotel on the place that catered for the coach passengers en route to Boulia and beyond. Also working on Woodstock was Harry Macrossan, who did a bit of prospecting for opal on the property. He had no real success, but dug a few holes around the station and picked up a bit of potch at Opal Lagoon. After Macrossan left Woodstock, Rigby became interested enough to do a bit of gouging in Macrossan's workings. He had no luck, although he did dig up a bit of potch at Opal Lagoon.

In about 1905 a man named Banning purchased Woodstock from Ellis and put a bore down near Bulbi Creek some time around 1911. Rigby, who had previously camped on the creek, moved to Bulbi bore. On a small hill that ran off the range beyond the bore, Rigby saw an eroded opal band. In his spare time he put down a couple of holes on the hill, without result, then dug a small open cut mine in the side of a gully that ran beside the hill. He is supposed to have found some opal in this open cut, but never continued working there. Rigby left Woodstock during the 1930s and retired to Charters Towers.

The mining of opal then virtually ceased in the areas around Winton for over 30 years. The Opalton and Windsor mineral fields were deserted, save for weekend fossickers looking for opal chips lost when the gougers were knapping stones. One man, Tom Pether, did dig for opal matrix (a mixture of stone and opal) on Carisbrook Station and Trevor Cluff also unearthed shallow boulder opal on his station, Franklin. It was no more than a hobby for Trevor, however. As a result of the inactivity on the opal fields, the mining warden at Winton was transferred. The Opalton mining area fell under the control of the Longreach warden, and Cloncurry was responsible for administering any mining in the Windsor mining field.

In 1961 four men set out from Kynuna to locate Rigby's diggings near Bulbi. In the party were Mick Cheadle, a stockman and prospector; Graham McKerrow, a grazier who had worked on Woodstock and knew the location of the mine; Rick Wallduck, a mate of Cheadle's; and Christy Black, an old timer from Kynuna who had been involved in opal mining in the early days. Two vehicles were taken: an ex-army blitz buggy owned by Mick, and Graham's ex-army jeep. The group first located Peter Karfe's old workings, where there were a couple of deep shafts and some shallow ones that had almost fallen in. Some good opal chips were found and it was obvious that good quality stones had been found there.

Above Kynuna the Diamantina River comes in from the south-west.

South of the river the country is exceedingly rough, with creeks like Glen George and Glen Urquhart running north to join the Diamantina. Despite having four-wheel drive vehicles, the going was very rough and some of the creeks tested the skill of the drivers and the quality of the vehicles. En route to Rigby's old mine the party visited the old Kynuna diggings; these shallow mines proved to be of little interest to the party, who then went on and camped on Glen Urquhart Creek. Next morning they found their way down the range that divided the watershed and arrived at Rigby's workings.

There was not a lot to be seen. The shallow holes on the hill were mostly fallen in and the small open cut was also badly eroded, but some faded chips of opal were found near the open cut. After looking around, the four men had lunch by the small creek that ran past the end of the hill. Graham was having generator trouble with the jeep so they decided to return via Woodstock Station, avoiding the rough country over the range.

Graham McKerrow wasn't interested in opal mining and returned to McKinlay, having played his part. Christy Black was too old to go gouging, but Mick Cheadle had caught the opal bug. Rigby's workings were to become the 'Red Flash' mining lease, the first mine to be worked full time since the collapse of the mining activities years before. The Red Flash produced gem-quality opal, and I was to become deeply involved in the mine.

The Opal Gouger's Lament

(Sung to the tune of the 'Girl I left behind me')

I've left the rat race far behind,
good luck to those who foller,
For I am down this flamin' shaft
a-gouging for a dollar.
The good life is for others now,
but I do not begrudge it,
For like a wombat underground,
I do not have a budget.

We work like hell upon this ridge,
for tucker to sustain us,
I've tightened up the windlass pipe
with washers from my anus.
We have no fridge upon this ridge,
the air is filled with thunder,
The food is rough and bad enough
to make a kelpie chunder.

The reds and blues of opal hues,
seduce me like a vision,
My duds and shirt are full of dirt,
thank God for circumcision.
There could be opal just ahead,
the thought is always nagging,
So I will strive to dig this drive
although my bottom's dragging.

To work like this without reward
a man must be a wanker,
I'm soaking wet with flamin' sweat,
my cheeks they run a banker.
But I am deep down underground
where the tax man cannot find me,
There's opal dirt on every side
and opal dirt behind me.

I've left the rat race far behind
and never wash my collar,
And I am starving slowly here
a-gouging for a dollar.
But when I climb this bloody shaft
at the nearest pub you'll find me.
There I'll have a beer and shed a tear
for the good life far behind me.

The Red Flash

By early 1963 the saddle repair shop I had established in Winton was doing well. I had not as yet sold my droving plant, but held no aspirations of returning to the stockroutes. Droving had been good to me, but with the trucks gaining an ever-increasing share of stock transport, the writing was on the wall. Besides, I was 39 years of age, and like most men I wanted some day to get married and have a family; the stockroutes were no place for a woman.

I had rented a shop opposite the council swimming pool from Gaynor Brushe and Sons, the plumbers. It had previously been the doctor's surgery and I often wondered about the privacy of consultations, for when Gaynor and his sons were building rainwater tanks, I had to shout to make myself heard. There could not have been too many medical secrets in Winton in those days. A Dr Ram had been the last medico to practise in the old surgery. There happened to be a spate of twin births in the little town during his time and the town wags used to go around chanting, 'Dr Ram will bring your lamb, two for the price of one.'

I used the back room, which had been the surgery, as a workroom, while in the waiting room I placed a counter and displayed some stock. One morning I was hard at work, when I heard someone enter the front of the shop. I went out to find a curly haired character of medium height holding a saddle. He heaved it onto the counter and said, 'Do you know what that is?'

I looked at him in surprise. 'Well,' I replied, 'it looks remarkably like a saddle.'

'Yeah, yeah, any bloody fool knows that. But what sort is it?'

I looked at his saddle carefully. 'Well, I'd say it's a Tim Carr, and without examining it I'd say it had a broken tree.'

The owner of the Carr saddle looked at me with grudging respect. 'OK, you know your saddles, but can you fix it?'

'No worries,' I told him, 'but I'll have to send away for a tree, and rasp a fair bit of it away to get it to fit.'

The curly headed ringer agreed and introduced himself as Mick Cheadle. He told me he had been running the camp on Yelvertoft Station near Mount Isa, but was now at Kynuna. He departed after telling me he would pick up the saddle in three weeks time. It was a rather inauspicious beginning to a lasting friendship and business relationship.

I obtained a tree and repaired the Carr saddle, but time went by and there was no sign of Mick Cheadle. Finally he strolled into my shop one day, ran his eyes over the saddle and paused. Then he said, 'I don't suppose you would take some opal for repairing it?'

I shook my head. 'Sorry, Mick ... Where did you get the opal?'

He snorted. 'You don't expect me to tell you that do you?'

'You mean you dug it yourself?'

'Bloody oath! I'm on to a good show.'

I thought for a while; opal had always fascinated me. I knew there had been no mining done around Winton for years and I was intrigued by Cheadle's remarks. 'Look, Mick, I may be able to help you later. Give me half the cost of repairing the saddle now, and I might look at some of your opal later.'

Mick went away rather relieved. I guessed he was finding opal mining a strain on his finances. I gave little more thought to Mick and his opal until he arrived at the shop a fortnight later. He showed me a parcel of rough opal. There was sand in some of the stones but the colour was excellent. I knew very little about opal at that time, but nevertheless I was impressed. Mick told me he was in half shares in the mine with Ron Brenton, but neither of them had any experience at marketing the opal. They had been selling large milk tins of poor quality rough to Harold Hurst, the Kynuna storekeeper, as tourist stones. This provided a bit of tucker money, but Harold wasn't interested in parcels of better quality opal. Mick said he and Ron felt they were not in a position to get a fair price for the gem-quality stones. After getting my assurance that anything he told me was confidential, Mick related to me the short history of the mine they were working.

After visiting Rigby's old claim with Graham McKerrow, he managed to get Ron Brenton interested in joining him in a mining venture. Ron was the Julia Creek to Kynuna mailman. Mick also enlisted the help of his mate, Rick Wallduck. After careful inspection of the old mine, Ron registered three mining leases, the Blue Speck, Opal Den and the Red Flash. The latter lease covered most of the old workings and was to be the one that would produce gem-quality opal. The group built a hut on the Blue Speck lease, constructed a windlass and started putting down a shaft on the hill. A primitive type of whip was also built using the old

Mick Cheadle, stockman and opal gouger, at the Red Flash mine, 1964. Photo: The author

lever and fulcrum system: a long pole is placed in a fork set in the ground; on the long end of this pole a lighter perpendicular pole is attached, to which the bucket is fastened; a rope on the short end allowed the bucket to be lowered, raised and swung to one side at the shaft head. One man worked the whip or windlass while his mate worked underground filling the bucket. These whips can still be seen in use in third world countries. Ladders were also used in working the Red Flash. As there was inadequate surface water available close to the Red Flash, 44 gallon drums were used to carry water up from the Bulbi bore.

Mick asked me if I would be interested in either buying the opal or alternatively acting as marketing agent for him and Ron. I told Mick I would like to see the mine and would give him a decision later. The following day Mick and I drove out through Woodstock Station to the Red Flash. There was not a lot to see but I was impressed by Mick's enthusiasm; I agreed to meet both partners in Winton to discuss a deal.

The meeting duly took place and I was offered a third share of production to market the opal. Mick, Ron and I were partners. Rick Wallduck was still working with Mick, and apparently they had some financial arrangement worked out between them. The first thing I did was to send the rough opal to Brisbane, where I had found a cutter willing to cut and polish the rough opal. When the cut stones came back they looked great to my uneducated eyes. Some were quite big, as heavy as 10 carats; I soon found out, however, that I had a lot to learn about the opal business.

General area around the Red Flash Mine. Photo: Peter Knowls

The Red Flash mine, with the whip in right foreground. Photo: Brian Holm

Opals should be cut to a standard size, ranging from one to three or four carats, so that setting the stones could be done at a reasonable cost. Only top quality gems warrant individual settings. Rather disillusioned, I sent the cut parcel to my brother Jeff, who was at that time working in Sydney. I had done a bit of homework and was aware that Sydney was the headquarters of the opal trade in Australia. It didn't take long for Jeff and I to find out just how hard it was to break into the business of selling opal. We talked on the phone and agreed that the stones should be cut again into regulation sizes. He was fortunate to obtain the services of a top cutter who was working for one of the biggest dealers in Sydney. He cut our opal in his spare time.

The freshly cut parcel was sold, although the price was a bit disappointing. Despite that, Mick and Ron were pleased; at last they had an outlet for their gem opal. Jeff played an important part in the marketing from that point on. Being in Sydney was a great advantage. By mid-year the mine was producing well and sales were being made overseas. I decided to register a company name to give our operations a more professional image, and the Capricornian Opal Company was duly registered at the Winton courthouse.

Capricornian Opal Company

Dealers and Exporters in Australian Opal

ELDERSLIE STREET - WINTON - QUEENSLAND

Phone : 311

Cable Address :

....

Letterhead of the Capricornian Opal Company

In August the Winton rodeo was held. The town was full of rodeo riders, station people and stockmen. Mick was in town, of course, as was Clive Teece, a mate of both Mick and mine.

Once the rodeo was over, someone organised a party out on Mistake Creek. Mick persuaded Clive to lend him his car and headed out. Mick loved a party, and it didn't bother him how rough it got. During the evening Mick and a rodeo rider had words, then got stuck into one another. Mick was no slouch with his fists, and to get a better view of proceedings some of the rodeo riders used Clive's car as a grandstand.

I knew nothing of this until next morning when an irate Clive found me at the Central Hotel. He invited me to inspect the roof of his car. I did so and commented that it looked as though a mob of billy goats had been dancing on it.

'It wasn't bloody billy goats, it was rodeo riders.'

He told me the story, and said Mick was too busy at the time to see who the culprits were. I felt sorry for Clive, for a generous gesture to a mate was going to cost him money, but I did not see what he wanted of me. I was soon to learn.

'I'm going to find the bastards that did this, and I need your help. Your know most of these rodeo blokes—we'll go round the pubs and question them.'

I knew it would be a futile exercise, but Clive was a mate of mine, so we set out on a search-and-destroy mission. It was, as I had suspected, a waste of time. Nobody knew anything, or if they did they weren't saying. Clive, who was usually a good natured chap, was getting progressively more hostile.

Finally I suggested to him that we give it away. He reluctantly agreed, but first we would have one more drink at the Australian Hotel. Like most of the pubs, the bar was crowded and Clive elbowed his way to the bar. As he reached it, he bumped against a chap in a black leather jacket, who turned to Clive and told him to f... off. Coming on top of the failed investigation, it was the last straw. Clive felled him like an ox.

The man in the leather jacket lay as though dead on the floor by the bar. On reaching for his beer, Clive almost fell over him.

'A man comes in for a quiet beer,' he complained, 'and he has to put up with bastards lying all over the place.' He turned to the barmaid. 'Why don't you get someone to drag the bludger out of here?'

He got short shrift from her. 'You knocked him down, drag him out yourself.'

We had another drink and left. As Clive drove me home I could see his humour had improved considerably. He hadn't found the culprits, but he'd had a victory of sorts.

I thought he would let the matter rest, but I could not have been more wrong. Next morning Clive turned up again, ready to continue the inquiry. I pointed out that it was a waste of time for us both, but Clive was adamant we could find the villains. He was a good mate so in the end I agreed to accompany him. As I expected, we had no more luck than on the previous day. At 11 o'clock Clive agreed it was hopeless and we dropped in to the North Gregory Hotel for a last drink before heading home.

Those days the North Gregory was a top hotel. It was owned by the Winton Council and managed by John Heads. We walked into the bar and ordered beers. By some twist of fate Clive found himself standing beside the man he had floored the day before. The man was minus the leather jacket, but was recognisable by his damaged face. Clive must have felt he had to say something.

'How are you going today?' he asked the man politely.

'Not bad, but I'd be a lot better if I could find the mongrel who king hit me yesterday,' was the reply.

'Oh, you would, eh? Well, your luck's in, you've found him.'

It was on again. The bar floor was tiled and Clive, who was wearing riding boots, slipped over. Sitting on the tiles, he pulled off a boot and flung it away. It headed straight for a glass shelf holding numerous bottles of spirits. John Heads leapt high and pulled off a spectacular one-handed catch. It would have extended Mark Taylor to the limit. By the time Clive had the other boot off, the situation was under control. Clive settled down, we drank our beers and departed. The investigation was over. Clive discovered his insurance would repair the car and everyone was happy.

The mining and marketing arrangements continued to work well until October 1963, when Ron Brenton, who had business interests elsewhere, sold me his half share in the Red Flash together with all the mining equipment. The leases had always been registered in Ron's name. From that point on the three leases—Nos. 5636, 5637 and 5667—were held in mine.

Mick and Rick carried on working the Red Flash mine, and production was steady. We now had a forwarding agent in Sydney to handle the parcels of opals we were exporting. Jeff took holidays from his job and was keen to get involved in mining the gemstones he had handled in Sydney. He came up to Winton and went out to the mine. He soon became an expert opal gouger.

By December the heat made mining difficult and the operation was shut down until after the wet. Jeff returned to Sydney and continued with marketing the opal. I planned to get married later in 1964, but at that time I was still in residence at the Central Hotel. I spent a rather boisterous festive season, but in preparation for my marriage I bought a block of land in Allen Street, and engaged Bobby Mann, a local carpenter, to build a modest home on the site.

Once weather conditions allowed, the mine started production again, Mick working on the open cut with some success. In May 1964 he asked me to buy his share of the Red Flash and Blue Spec leases. The Red Flash was the only lease of the three to produce opal. Mick kept a share in the Opal Den lease, and Ron retained his shares in both the Blue Spec and in Opal Den. It was more to remain involved than anything else; those leases had never shown signs of being worth working—holes drilled with the extended auger had drawn a blank. As a result, their sale price was virtually nil.

Jeff now left his job in Sydney, as contacts with buyers were well established. He joined Mick in working the Red Flash on a share of opal produced. By then Rick had given the opal gouging away and returned to stockwork.

Jeff and Mick got on very well together. A good working relationship is absolutely essential when two men are thrown together in an isolated situation. Mick had then been working at the Red Flash for over 12 months, and Jeff and I were aware he was getting itchy feet. Mick is a born prospector, always eager to see what is over the next hill. To ease the monotony of mining, the pair would go off prospecting for a day or two. The Red Flash was not far from where Brennen's claim must have

Windlass on shaft at the Red Flash mine. Photo: Brian Holm

been and the fact that the long lost mine may well be close was a constant challenge to Mick.

Sometimes if money was late arriving from buyers, I made an advance from my bank account to cover costs. On these occasions, Mick, who had a lively sense of humour, used to call me 'Mr Big'. He would inspect the depleted tucker box, turn to Jeff and say, 'I fear we must go to town and put the fangs into Mr Big.'

It was about this time that Mick and Jeff received a visit from a rather odd character. He was driving an almost brand new LandRover and informed them he was a dogger employed by the council. He raved on about firearms and showed the pair a .44 automatic pistol he had planted under the seat of the vehicle. After he had departed, Mick decided they would need to keep an eye on the dogger, declaring, 'That bastard could knock us off for our opals.'

It wasn't an outlandish statement. The Red Flash was in an isolated spot, miles from anywhere. Jeff agreed, and the next time the dogger drove up to the mine Mick met him on his own.

'Where's your mate?' asked the visitor.

'You can't see him,' replied Mick. 'But he's over there with a rifle pointed at your guts.'

The dogger did not wait around. He put the LandRover into gear and departed at great speed. Mick, who always saw the funny side of things, thought it was a great joke.

They only saw the dogger once more. There was a rough road down the range behind the mine. One morning Mick and Jeff heard an engine at full revs, and over the top of the range, well away from the road, came the dogger. The LandRover was ricocheting from rock to rock and colliding into trees, and before the eyes of the startled pair, it began to shed bits and pieces as it tore down the descent. The dogger was thrown about like a rag doll, but was still clinging to the wheel of the battered vehicle when it hit the bottom. The LandRover was hardly recognisable. The hood was gone and the mudguards were hanging loose. Without a glance at the opal miners, the dogger accelerated away, shedding parts of the vehicle as he went.

The pair worked the mine almost up to Christmas, then spent the festive season in Kynuna, and then, rather the worse for wear, returned to the mine. The wet season brought them into Winton for a well-earned respite. Production from the Red Flash had been good, new shafts had been put down and the old open cut had yielded some very good opals.

Opals from the Red Flash mine. Photo: Peter Knowls

We were now forwarding parcels of rough opal to overseas destinations on a fairly regular basis.

The government's policy on levying sales tax on opal left me wondering about the collective brain power of politicians. Australia is the only country in the world that produces gem-quality opal that will stand cutting. To sell a cut stone, however, 25 per cent sales tax must be added, while as much rough opal as you wish can be sent overseas tax free. It's much the same with most of our primary industries. Instead of encouraging the adding of value to what we produce, we ship it abroad for others to make money out of by processing the raw materials. We then commit an even greater folly by buying back the finished products.

While in Winton Jeff bought a Willy's jeep tray body truck, and as soon as the weather allowed he returned to the mine. Mick stayed on working the Red Flash under a new agreement for some months, after which Jeff mined it on his own until the end of the year. I cannot say I was all that keen on the idea, but Jeff wasn't at all worried about it. To be truthful, being newly married, I was not keen to join him, besides I had my hands full at the shop, a business that could, if required, provide financial support for the mining venture. My brother is one of those unusual characters who can work quite well with others, but is in his element when operating on his own.

A lot of station owners and managers resent the presence of prospectors and miners on their property. We were fortunate that the manager of Woodstock, Alex Logan was a gentleman. Realising the mine was in an isolated location, he did everything possible to help. I knew Alex quite well, as he was one of the stalwarts of the Diamantina Devils cricket club.

Jeff produced some very good parcels of opals during 1965. By the end of the year, though, Jeff and I decided to cease full-time work at the Red Flash. Over the previous three years the mine had produced a lot of top quality opal, but in Jeff's opinion more ground would have to be opened up to maintain production. We agreed we were in no position to carry out expansion at that time.

During the early part of 1966 Brian Holm and his mate Ron Norris did weekend share mining at the Red Flash. On some occasions, Brian's grandfather, Fred Holm, accompanied them. Fred had been on the Opalton diggings in the field's heyday. Clive Edmonstone and Ron

Fred Holm inspecting opal-bearing sandstone at the Red Flash mine.
Photo: Brian Holm

McKenzie also did a bit of work at the mine. In May 1966 I sold a major interest in the three leases to Ron.

The mining boom began soon after and the stock exchange went berserk. A company was floated in the South with nothing more than an authority to prospect over a large area around the old Opalton field. A parcel of shares was allocated to the local people, but I refused to subscribe to a company that could offer no more than a map of an ATP area. The shares went onto the market at a high price and a lot of people made a quick quid. The poor devils who bought shares and held them got their fingers burnt; the company folded without putting a hole down. I could have made money at someone else's expense, but my principles will probably keep me poor until the day I die.

Towards the end of the mining boom, Ron and I were approached by a group with an offer to buy the Red Flash. They planned to float a company called I.B.I.S. Mining NL. The proposed company had plans to lease other promising areas, and seemed genuinely interested in long-term opal mining. I knew some of the people involved in the company and was fully satisfied with their bona fides.

By the time the company was ready to float, however, the boom was

Brian Holm at the top of the old shaft at the Red Flash mine. Photo: Brian Holm

I.B.I.S. Mining N.L.
(Incorporated 1970)

All correspondence
to be addressed to:
THE SECRETARY,
P.O. Box 840,
Ingham, Q., 4850

Phone: Ingham 1044

Registered Office:
91 LANNERCOST STREET,
INGHAM, Q., 4850

15th October, 1970

Mr B. Simpson,
Elderslie St.,
Winton

Mr R. Mc Kenzie,
Matilda Caravan Park,
Winton

Dear Sir,

This is to confirm our verbal undertaking to purchase from you your claims comprising the Red Flash mine for a sum of four thousand dollars, such sale to be affected after the Company has carried out its planned expansion of capital.

Yours faithfully,

W. S. CUMMINGS
SECRETARY

Letter of confirmation from I.B.I.S. Mining NL

over and mining shares were no longer the flavour of the month; as a result, the float was under-subscribed. I.B.I.S., unlike its namesake, never got off the ground.

The Red Flash was the first opal mine to be worked full time in the area for many years. More importantly it revived interest in the old opal diggings around Winton. Before I left Winton I sold my remaining interest in the mine to the late Vince Evert. Vince went on to become one of the pioneers of the new opal boom. Within a few short years Mayne Side and Opalton were again hives of industry.

On the Banks of the Outer Barcoo

Today is the Sabbath, the last in the week,
  A day of devotion and rest.
But there's no morning service and no 'Salvo' band
  For the toilers who work in the West.
Down in the city they're off to the beach
  Or have taken the kids to the zoo.
There are no like attractions around about here
  On the banks of the outer Barcoo.

Now sport is ideal for passing the time,
  Thus putting in part of the day,
But when one had neither opponents nor gear
  It's a bit hard to know what to play.
We couldn't play cricket or tennis or bowls,
  We've neither a draught board nor cue,
And never a golf club or caddy we've seen
  On the banks of the outer Barcoo.

Now shooting, they say, is a very fine sport,
  With that we are forced to agree,
But the only firearm that we have in the camp
  Was made in the last century.
The barrel's cut short and its blasting report
  Can be heard from here to the Loo,
And a most lethal shock is got from the stock
  If one shoots on the outer Barcoo.

We've tried our hand fishing down by the big bend,
  For a big feed of fish would be nice,
But never a word from the fish have we heard
  Though we've dropped them a line once or twice.
We've sat on our tail never seeing a scale,
  Though the mossies were biting, it's true,
But the fish don't approve of the bait that we use
  On the banks of the outer Barcoo.

Now down in the city when Sunday comes round
  And you're off to the footie or club,
Give a second's thought then to the poor working men
  Who are stuck away out in the scrub.
When it's all said and done it isn't much fun,
  Though whingeing with us is taboo,
But hop on your bike and see what it's like
  On the banks of the outer Barcoo.

Bush Entertainment

My mate Bruce Hanson and I once took a couple of girls to the pictures in Camooweal. The 'theatre' was no more than a rectangular galvanised iron fence with a fibro screen erected at one end and a projection box at the other. The projector was turned by hand, and as the projectionist's arm grew tired, action in the film would slow then jerk and speed up as he changed hands. But it was somewhere to go, so in we went and sat down on the canvas-covered deckchairs that were placed in rows on the stony ground. The film was a run of the mill affair, with cowboys and Indians chasing one another across the screen. Then came the part where the immigrant train circled the wagons against an impending Indian attack. The braves were shown lined up on a nearby hill, then the chief rode forward and the camera zoomed in to give a close up of him sitting arrogantly on his horse. At that moment a hard case in the audience bent down and, picking up a stone, threw it with unerring aim at the screen. The missile took the chief's head clean off his shoulders, and left a hole the size of a basketball in the fibro screen. The offender was hustled out amid laughter, boos and whistles; for me it was the highlight of the evening.

The introduction of television and videos to the bush radically changed the social life of its people. Movie going was once one of the main sources of entertainment. Every town had its picture theatre; many of the outback ones were open air shows, but that was of little consequence as it seldom rained out there and when it did it was always welcome. Few of these theatres have survived the invasion of technology. One that has is the Royal Theatre in Winton. A partly open air building, it has been owned and operated by the Evert family for three generations. During its early days it survived a fire, and doubled for a boxing ring and a skating rink. Of late it has become the popular venue for 'The Poets' breakfast' during the Winton festivals. The Royal Theatre still puts on two shows a week during the tourist season. Long may it defy the idiot box.

Once when I was trucking bullocks in Dajarra, I found the Australian Inland Mission vehicle had arrived in the little trucking town. Word spread that the padre would put on a picture show that night, and the town kids were delighted. Rather than drink at the pub, I decided to join them at the show. The projector was set up in the street, with the side of the galvanised iron storeroom acting as the screen, and everyone brought along their own chairs. I forget what the picture was, but I thoroughly enjoyed myself; the kids did too. They were fascinated by the way the actors made their undulating way across the corrugated iron screen.

In the days before couch potatoes and push button entertainment, people had to amuse themselves. This was even more critical in the bush; city people have always had the edge on their country cousins where entertainment is concerned. The denizens of the bush managed to amuse themselves quite adequately, however, and they did so for the most part without the aid of strong drink—the ubiquitous stubby had not then become an Australian icon. Unmarried stockmen and drovers did drink, of course, but for the most part this was a short spree after months in the bush.

When I was a youngster, family picnics were always popular. I have vivid recollections of picnics on Cattle Creek with my family friends. Our respective parents would recline on rugs spread under the paperbarks and talk of whatever parents discussed in those days. Meanwhile, we kids would swim in the clear waters, sail makeshift boats and play 'make believe' games in the scrub that bordered the sandy reaches.

Children back then had to rely more on themselves for amusement, and as a result they learned to use their imagination rather than to depend on provided diversions. A child's imagination is a treasure house, a veritable fantasy land. Children who utilise the gift of youthful imagination are seldom bored.

Tennis has always been played in the country. There was a lot of small bush schools about in the past and most of them had a court, usually built from an ant bed. This was collected from white ant nests and puddled to provide an excellent playing surface. Most of the school courts were home to adult tennis clubs and as a result the school became the hub of local social life. Many of the bigger stations, particularly in the sheep country, had their own courts and station tennis afternoons were popular social occasions.

Everyone could dance in the days before television and every little town had a hall of some sort where the local dances were held. The country state schools were also pressed into service for these events. Most were on high stumps, and when a dance was planned, the desks

Tennis in the Outback 1920 style. Photo: the late Don Simpson

and forms were taken underneath, the cracks in the floorboards were filled with candle grease, and a mixture of sawdust and kero was broadcast. The result was a satisfactorily fast surface. I rode to many of those dances as a youth and enjoyed myself immensely. The girls would sit along one wall while their mothers played euchre in the supper room, with one eye on their cards the other on their daughters. Getting musicians for these dances was never a problem—the country seemed to be full of them. Once could dance with a girl then and whisper sweet nothings in her ear if one desired: to converse with your partner at today's discos, a man would need semaphore flags or a megaphone.

Country dances ranged from the schoolroom hops to the grand race and woolshed balls of the outback. Those balls were splendid affairs at which the ladies would be resplendent in ball gowns, with up-to-date hairstyles. These functions were good news for the business houses in the Western towns. Graziers had money back then and the local dress shops and hairdressers welcomed the ball season. Unfortunately, class distinction was alive and well years ago in the sheep country. At one town, at least, a rope was put across the hall at the balls, the grazing fraternity dancing in splendid isolation at one end of the hall, and the townsfolk and workers at the other.

Social gathering at Isis Woolshed, 1920. Photo: the late Don Simpson

Happily, this obnoxious practice has disappeared from the West. I organised a rather remarkable dance once in Camooweal. My mate Bruce Hanson and I were waiting for the season to break in 1952, so a couple of girls we knew persuaded us to put on a dance. We agreed and Bruce left the arrangements to me. I booked the shire hall at the council office and found a lady who played the piano and a ringer who could play the drums. The big night came and, as there was no door charge, a good crowd was soon dancing to lively music. Shortly after 10 o'clock the local sergeant of police came into the hall. He must have asked who was in charge, for he came over to me. The sergeant was a well-liked bloke and I wondered what the trouble was.

He drew me to one side and said, 'I'm afraid you'll have to stop the dance.'

'Stop the dance! It's just getting warmed up. Why?'

He pushed his cap back and scratched his head. 'Well, I've just got word that King George the Sixth has died. I think you had better stop as a mark of respect.'

I reluctantly agreed, although I doubt if Buckingham Palace would have worried too much about our activities. I went over and told the musicians to stop playing, then announced the news to the assembled dancers. They accepted the closure with good grace, although I suspected some were more upset about the cancellation of the dance than about the death of their monarch. Bruce and I turned off the lights and closed the hall doors on a memorable evening.

At one time hotels in the country had billiard rooms with a permanently employed billiard marker to look after them. The bush produced some outstanding players at both billiards and snooker as a result, and Jack Howard of Boulia is reputed to have been a player almost as skilled as the great Walter Lindrum Most mothers warned their sons about these billiard rooms, calling them dens of iniquity, no doubt in response to the illegal gambling that went on in them. This was a matter for the local police to control, of course, and raids were sometimes made, but the results were never spectacular.

Usually one man ran the gambling in the billiard rooms, and games like crown and anchor, inns and outs and two-up or swy were favourites. In Winton the man who ran the gambling school was Wicky Taylor. Wicky was a respected character of the town. He could fight like a thrashing machine and his wits were as fast as his fists. He usually ran a game of two-up on Sunday mornings, the venue a spot behind Elliot's dairy, just behind the present Waltzing Matilda Centre. Being careful of his reputation, Wicky always employed the services of a cockatoo, or look-out. On one particular morning the game was progressing in a satisfactory manner, the heads of the crowd raising and lowering as eyes followed the flight of the pennies. Unfortunately the look-out must have been dozing, for Wicky looked up to see the police almost upon him.

'Quick! Pick up your money,' Wicky hissed. In one quick movement he slipped the kip and pennies into his pocket and pulled out a dog-eared bible.

'Raise up your eyes to the Lord, brothers,' he cried, at the same time throwing his arm in the air.

'Now let us pray.' Wicky lowered his head and the crowd did likewise.

As the police arrived, Wicky held out a hand. 'Welcome to our little prayer meeting. Brother Bates will be taking the hat around in a minute, please give generously.'

It was a masterful performance. The baffled police left before the hat reached them and the game continued.

The racing game has always had a large following in the outback. Meetings ranged from the corn-fed meetings in the larger towns to picnic races in smaller ones, where grass-fed horses carried the colours of their owners. Bookmakers usually attended these meetings, but the odds they offered were nothing to write home about. Two of these bush race meetings, Brunette and Birdsville, have become notable successes. The Brunette races have retained much of their original character, but the Birdsville meeting has unfortunately become a venue for yuppies.

Problems with race fixing, doping and other dubious practices have been a common feature of the racing game worldwide, and the outback has never been any different. At a meeting in the Gulf years ago the jockey on the favourite was told to pull the horse—that is, prevent it from winning. The horse's connections had put a large wager on another starter and hoped to make a killing.

The jockey followed orders, but the horse had other ideas. It came down the home straight lengths in front of the field, almost pulling its rider's arms out of their sockets in the process. Realising that his mount could not be beaten, the jockey promptly dropped the reins and fell off. The horse was of course disqualified, the connections won the money and all was well.

For those punters who followed the sport of kings from afar, there were always SP bookies in every town to cater for their habit. Although this type of betting was illegal, little was ever done to stamp out the practice.

Rodeos were also popular annual events in the bush. I was associated with the sport for some time in Winton, acting as shute boss and later as judge. Those days the buckjumpers were brought up from stations like Springvale; most of them would buck a town down and their style was quite unpredictable. They spun, bucked high, shoulder bucked and chopped. They were a real test of a horseman's ability.

Mount Isa was the last major rodeo in Queensland to buck its own horses. Under pressure from rodeo 'cowboys', though, the committee will now be using contract stock only. The horses provided by these contractors are known to the riders and have only one style of bucking—straight ahead while kicking up. Rodeos have certainly changed. Horsemen have become 'cowboys' who ride in big American saddles, and buckjumpers are now 'broncos'. Give me the old days when men who looked like Australians rode really bad horses in small Australian saddles.

Stockmen who worked in the cattle camps years ago had to rely entirely on their initiative for entertainment. There were no radios in those days and newspapers were virtually unknown in the camps. Sports were held and even after a hard day's branding, ringers lined up for broad jumping, backwards jumping and various other athletic diversions. Other contests were held, too, such as one which involved toeing the line and, with one hand on the ground, placing a match box out as far as possible with the other. A variation of this was to place the matchbox between the teeth while balancing on the hands with the knees placed on the elbows. We had some weird and wonderful events, but they helped to pass the time. At night we yarned, recited and played mouth organs, the only musical instrument we could carry in a swag. At times we played cards—poker mostly, for matches, as we had little cash with us.

At times we played a game called 'yarding the bull'. Like noughts and crosses, it was a game that usually ended without result; however, it could be won if one of the players lost concentration. It was usually played with the game board scratched on the ground in this fashion:

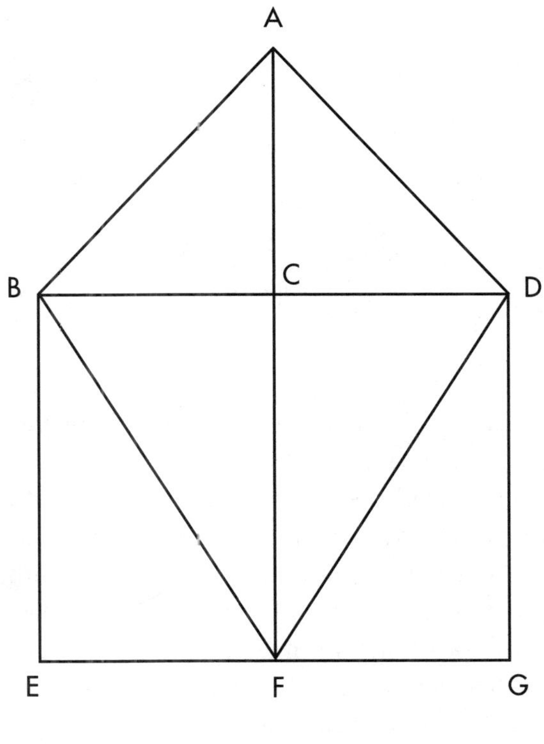

The idea was to yard the bull to position A, with the horsemen at positions B, C and D. The game starts with the bull at position C and the horsemen at positions E, F and G. The bull must move first. The bull can either be yarded or can escape by reaching any of the positions marked E, F or G.

The Aboriginal stockmen used to play a far more difficult game that needed a lot of mental concentration. A diagram like this was made in the dirt.

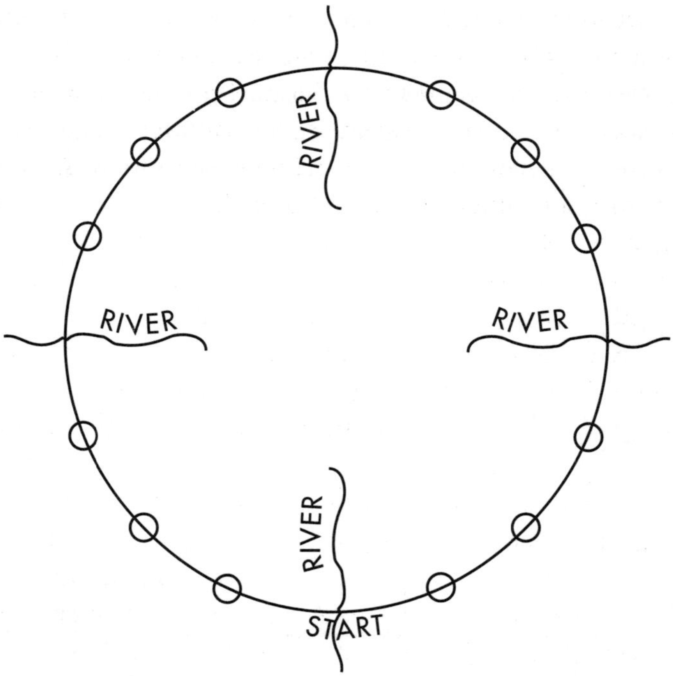

This game is played by having a caller ask the player, who is blindfolded, to nominate each position by asking, 'What's here?'. The player starts by answering, 'river' then 'nothing', 'nothing', 'nothing', 'river', as the caller questions him. When he has gone round the board to the starting river once, he must then put a man on the first 'nothing' space. He then continues putting one man on the next space at each round of the board. When all the positions are manned, he must then remove a man at each round of the board until the 'nothing' spaces are empty again. This goes on until the player makes a mistake.

I have tried this game and it is very challenging indeed. A player must retain a clear mental picture of the game board at all times. I was never as good at it as some of the Aborigines.

There was, of course, a lot of well-organised sport played in the more heavily populated area of the outback. In the sheep country the grazing fraternity played polo, while the less affluent tried their hands at polocrosse, a game resembling la cross but played on horses. Polocrosse never really prospered as polo did.

Rugby League was always a favourite with both players and spectators. In the Central West, the local competition was a high-profile affair played between the towns of Tambo, Barcaldine, Blackall, Longreach and Winton. Paid players and coaches from the South were engaged regularly, and at times ex-international players schooled the teams. As a result the standard of play was close to that of city clubs.

Travel, although arduous, was never a problem. The team from Tambo and its supporters would leave home early Sunday morning, travel to Winton, play a hard-fought game that afternoon, indulge in a few drinks afterwards and then drive back to Tambo, a round trip of 970 kilometres. Very few city teams could stand that pace. Next day the Tambo lads would be back in the shearing sheds, work that contributed a great deal to their toughness.

I doubt if anything could be further removed from droving than the grand old game of cricket. However, during its heyday as a drovers' town, Camooweal prided itself on having quite a respectable (I use the term loosely) cricket team. Over the summer months when droving was done, I had an occasional game with them, as did others who, like me, had fallen under the spell of the willow in earlier days and in far distant places. As we invariably played in temperatures of around 40°C, the organisers of our games, conscious of the grave dangers of dehydration, were generous in the provision of liquid refreshment. This, of course, was vital for replacing the bodily fluids lost in the pursuit of leather. It was an admirable precaution but made winning the toss imperative, for the life-preserving fluid affected our batting far more than our bowling. If we batted first, we usually put together a respectable total. If, however, unkind fate decreed that we should go to the crease second, a batting collapse was inevitable. It was of no use looking to the lower order to restore our fortunes; the tail never wagged. By the time the tail enders were due to bat, they had difficulty finding their way to the wicket, let alone striking the ball.

To say that the Camooweal cricket ground was rough would be a gross understatement. We did have a concrete pitch, but the outfield was totally devoid of grass and was littered with stones far larger than the ball we used. The ground was dragged before each game, but it made little difference—new stones were unearthed as the top ones were removed. Nothing could get rid of them. The Barkly Tableland Shire Council, at that time based in the drovers' town, admitted defeat. On most cricket fields the course of a cover drive is reasonably predictable. It wasn't like that on the Camooweal ground. There the ball was likely to rear up off a stone and strike the startled fieldsman smartly between the eyes. Fortunately, due to the life-preserving fluids we felt little pain.

The Camooweal eleven sometimes travelled to Mount Isa to play social cricket against the teams there. We played on a field at Spear Creek that was later to become the Mount Isa rodeo grounds. On one memorable occasion we played a team from the town's post office. They were a genial bunch who did not take the game too seriously, and as a result the beer flowed like bore water and a good time was had by all.

I forget who won the match; somehow it did not seem all that important at the time. What was unusual was that one of our members who never drank let his head go and became as blind as a bat. It may have been the weather or the lively company, we never found out. When the time came to depart he was legless and had to be helped into a car, where he promptly went to sleep.

On the way back to Camooweal we all pulled up for a comfort stop at Inca Creek. Our drunken mate woke, lurched out and leapt into a muddy waterhole by the road. There he wallowed about like a water buffalo, muttering, 'Gotta sober up or the missus will kill me.' He was finally persuaded to come out, looking more like the creature from the black lagoon than a cricketer. No driver wanted the mud-covered inebriate in his vehicle, but the problem was solved by rolling him up cocoon-like in the long cricket mats. He was snoring loudly when we reached Camooweal. Pulling up at his house, we unrolled him on the front lawn, then waved and sped away as his wife opened the front door.

During the years I spent in Winton I became heavily involved in cricket; the game was enjoying a period of intense popularity in the West. The town teams took part in a three-cornered contest as well as playing

GEORGINA TIMES

THE OFFICIAL ORGAN OF THE CAMOOWEAL CRICHET CLUB
VOL.1 ISSUE No 5.

THE GRAND OPENING OF THE CAMOOWEAL CRICKET OVAL

Reports on the opening ceremony and the days cricket.

The Oval was offically opened by the Chairman of the Barkly Tablelands Shire Council on Sunday the 23rd October, 1955, who congratulated the Cricket Club on their enterprise in providing the Oval not only for Cricket but also for general sporting activities.

The first over was bowled by Pop Finlay to Jack Dawson. No runs nor wickets were taken. The only thing nearly taken was the wicket keepers head.

A scratch match was played on that day between teams Captained by Squash Perry and G. Trembath .Squash won the toss, and elected to bat. The innings was opened by F.Martin and Doug Milne. Milne was caught by Tait bowled by Sheehey for a duck. Martin was then joined by Holt and with the score at 47 Martin retired after scoring 22 runs. Ormonde was the next batsman but was out very smartly for another duck. Caught by the mighty Steene, Bowled Tait. Buchanan then joined Holt and together they took the score to 110 before Holt was caught and bowled for 52. Which included 8,4's this was the highest score on both sides. Simpson was the new bat-sman joining Buchanan who was later given out. L.B.W. to Trembath. (Umpire. J. Ormonde). After this the tail did its best to wag but the innings closed at 136.

Sheehey and Burke opened for Trembaths 11, where they scored 43 runs between them before Burke was caught Perry bowled Holt for 15. Freckleton then joined Sheehey, but was soon out for 2. bowled by F.Martin. Tait was the next batsman, but had a change of partner soon after. Sheehey was bowled by Holt for 29. Trembath then faced the bowler making 5. Bunny then entered the wicket and made 6. Steene made 11. Rooke then joined Tait but only three runs were added before Tait was caught. F.Martin. Bowled D.Milne 42. runs being made which included 2. 6's and 3 4's Rooke made 15. before he was stumped by Buchanan off Perry. A few more runs were made by the remaining players before the innings clos-ed giving Trembaths 11 victory by 9 runs.

social cricket with country sides. Representative teams also played against elevens from Muttaburra, Hughenden and Longreach. These rep games were taken very seriously. The arch enemy was Longreach, against whom we played for the Speed Myers' trophy.

One of the chaps who played with my town team was a rather difficult chap to handle—difficult, that is, on the cricket field or in a brawl. He was a fast bowler who hated batsmen almost as much as he disliked policemen. We shall call him Frank. Frank's bowling was very fast indeed, his speed only being exceeded by his lack of direction. Now and again, however, he bowled the unplayable ball. On one occasion a Winton rep team played an away game at Muttaburra. On inspecting the concrete pitch, we found that it was covered by coir, or coconut matting. Now, coir is quite springy and usually helps spin bowlers, and we found it certainly added pace to Frank's deliveries.

Muttaburra won the toss and decided to bat. When all was ready, the captain tossed the ball to Frank to open the bowling. As he walked back to his mark, the man at mid-off told him the batsman facing up was a policeman. This put the opener in double jeopardy. Frank turned with a light in his eye that was enough to make strong men shudder. I was fielding in the covers, but I never saw the ball Frank bowled, it was so fast. It must have landed just short of a length. It came off the coir like greased lightning, striking the unfortunate batsman on the forehead. He went down as though shot and was carried off unconscious. We apologised for the incident and the game continued. Frank's bowling became normal again, his next ball almost taking first slip's head off, then going screaming to the boundary for four byes.

Of all the social cricket we played, the games I enjoyed most were against the Diamantina Devils, a team of bushmen from the Channel Country stations. They were a great group of sportsmen whose home ground was a huge claypan at Munduran Station. It was almost as hard as concrete, and as fast as a skating rink. If a ball penetrated the field, it went like a flash, not only to the boundary, but seemingly to the horizon. A fieldsman virtually needed a fast horse and a cut lunch to retrieve it. The cricket mats were pegged down straight onto the natural surface, which always stayed firm, and a clump of gidgee trees on the edge of the claypan served as a grandstand, dressing room and bar. The ladies from 'down the river' always put on a slap-up lunch and after the game we ate our fill of good local beef, cooked using a large circular saw blade as a barbecue plate.

After the meal everyone had to take a turn at entertaining the crowd. By popular demand two items never varied at these after-game festivities. Phil Cluff always sang 'The road to Mandalay', and then he would play a gumleaf while his brother Trevor did a tapdance on the upturned barbecue plate.

Whether true or not, the Diamantina Devils always told us they had a proper constitution. Rule 42 of this document forbade players to engage in sex the night before a game. They also said there used to be a rule 43 advising players not to engage in this pastime after a match. With broad grins, we were told that this rule was struck out as it was found to be unnecessary. Every match against the Diamantina Devils was a memorable affair.

Cricket is the greatest game of all. It is played worldwide by many different people, but no one plays the game with more zest and enjoyment than the 'flannelled fools' of the outback.

The Quartpot Maiden

Out further West some time ago when fashion favoured laces,
The day arrived in Quartpot Town to hold the yearly races.
From miles around the bushmen came to pass a friendly greeting
And try to take each other down and clean up on the meeting.
The program was designed to woo the local racing gentry,
And for the 'plum', the maiden plate, there was a record entry,
For nominations numbered four—a mighty field and classy,
From sandhill runs beyond they came—from paddocks lush and grassy.

The bush crowd lined the Quartpot course, a crooked mile and tricky,
A blue-bush swamp just past the turn was sometimes rather sticky.
But little did they care for that, to them it had small meaning,
Nor did they mind the crazy way the judge's box was leaning.
One bookie came to rob the crowd and bribe the leading rider
And from his odds, a crippled goat was scarcely an outsider.
From off a box he laid the field, his voice was far from mellow,
The wire and sapling members' stand vibrated to his bellow.

Now Mulga Lad, a likely colt, was fast though rather tender;
The hoop engaged for Wallaroo was still upon a bender.
The Spider had a chance, some said, a smart and trusted starter,
But favourite for the maiden was a filly known as Garter.
A cunning field they were, no doubt, some 'stung', some dead as Caesar,
The ancient stipe who checked them out could scarce see past his sneezer.
And while the judge drank twenty rums to banish indecision
He read a girlie magazine to fortify his vision.

The field lined up, the starter raised an old and rusted Snider,
The shot he fired to start the race wrote finis to the Spider.
The rest took off along the track o'er stony ground and ridgey,
And soon were lost to public sight behind a clump of gidgee.
Around the turn and up the straight the field was next seen speeding
And by a length, or so it seemed, that Mulga Lad was leading.
In wild abandonment he raced, the dirt and gravel throwing,
His laboured breathing as he rolled was like a grampus blowing.

Now Garter racing close behind, the inside too was hogging,
At every stride her crooked hoop the leader's rump was flogging.
Just then upon the narrow track, his master's oaths unheeding,
There strayed a canine specimen of rather doubtful breeding.
With tail a-jaunt he jogged along, gaze fixed on post and railing;
All efforts to avoid a smash were futile—unavailing,
For Mulga Lad leapt o'er the fence while Garter legged it after,
And Wallaroo bucked through the stand amid the hoots and laughter.

The hound, ignoring totally the havoc he was causing,
Changed his mind and trotted by the post not even pausing.
Then from his box the drunken judge, his bleary eyeballs shadin',
Declared that Mick Malaney's dog had won the Quartpot Maiden.
And still today they tell the tale and never lack a hearing
In public bars, in drovers' camps, in sheds when they are shearing,
For in our outback history an epic never fadin'
Occurred in Quartpot Town the day a sheep dog won the Maiden.

North to the Gulf

The bar of the Australian Hotel was crowded with bushmen—men who after a year's hard work in the outback were down in Brisbane letting off steam. It was a noisy session as yarns, jokes, exaggerated claims and downright lies floated around the bar. It was a strange place, the old Australian, known to most of us as Mulga Corner. The beer served there was not our favourite drop, yet it drew us all like a magnet. The hotel was on the corner of Queen and Albert streets, but once inside you could have been in any bush pub in the outback.

I was drinking with a mate of mine, Jack Britt. We had worked together in stockcamps and on the road droving. I had run into Jack a few days before, and not having seen him for over two years, we found plenty to talk about. There was a burst of laughter down the bar and I looked over to see Big Jack Stead trying to win the heart of one of the barmaids. Jack was from Quilpie and, like most of us those days, his technique with women was fairly basic; but the girl handled his approaches with the ease and aplomb gained from long experience with amorous bushmen. She was missing a great opportunity, Steady told her, then returned to drinking beer with his mates. I ordered a couple more drinks and when they arrived I told Jack I was thinking of heading back bush. He looked at me. 'Where do you reckon you'll go, back to the Territory?'

I had spent the last two years in the Channel Country and I felt I needed a change. 'I'm not sure, Jack. I've been giving some thought to the Gulf.'

'Well, mate, if you're not certain, the best thing is to toss a coin.'

He picked up a penny from the change on the bar. 'Right, it's heads the Gulf, tails the Territory.' Britty tossed the coin in the air, caught it and, without looking at it, slapped it on his wrist. He removed his hand, and there it was, a head. I would try my luck on the stations in the Gulf of Carpentaria. I was quite happy with the decision-making process. It may seem a bit harum-scarum, but we were a carefree lot those days, quite happy to accept whatever might befall us.

Jack and I had a couple more beers then crossed Queen Street to the Central cafe. We sat down and ordered a traditional meal of ham and eggs with mashed vegetables. Over lunch Jack and I yarned about the

Gulf Country and the best areas to work in. I had already decided to go to Cloncurry and pick up a job ringing there. I was happy about the decision because it would give me an opportunity to see my mother. She was now living in Mackay and I could break my journey there for a few days. I had not seen her for over two years. My youngest brother, Jeff, was still at school, but we three older ones were a footloose lot. I knew my mother worried a lot about us, but it was not until years later, when I had children of my own, that I realised just how many of her grey hairs we must have been responsible for.

After Jack and I finished our meal, we shook hands and wished each other good luck. I then walked down to the tourist bureau and booked a rail ticket to Cloncurry. It would be a long trip, first of all up to Townsville on the Cairns Mail, then out to Cloncurry on the train to Mount Isa. That night I threw my swag into the luggage compartment of the northern mail train and settled back in a seat. It was goodbye to the bright lights and back to work.

I broke my journey at Mackay and after three very pleasant days there I again caught the northbound mail train. Although it was early April, the wet season was not yet over and the rain bucketed down during the night. I expected the Burdekin to be over the bridge, so was pleasantly surprised when the train puffed across with some leeway between the tracks and the rising floodwater. Our good fortune was too good to last, though, and washouts further north brought the train to a lengthy stop. When the Cairns Mail finally pulled in to the station at Townsville it was close to midnight. Cramped from the long journey, I retrieved my swag and waited for the platform to clear.

The train pulled out after a few minutes, and very soon everyone had departed. I shouldered my swag and walked to the end of the roofed platform, where I dropped the swag on the concrete. The rain gleamed in the station lights and lashed down on the railway lines while the wind moaned in the overhead wires and swept down the deserted platform. It was at best a very dismal night. I shivered slightly and rolled my sleeves down, buttoning them at my wrists. This situation didn't bother me for I had my swag and, to a bushman, his swag is virtually his home. Sitting on my haunches, I unbuckled the straps around my swag and unrolled it. The contents were rather basic. A large pocket held my clothes and other gear, and acted as a pillow. The swag contained two well-worn blankets but no mattress. The concrete would be hard, but I had slept on hard surfaces before and was tired enough to sleep on a barbed wire fence. Pulling off my boots, I placed them beside my whip and lay back, pulling my hat over my eyes.

I was almost asleep when I heard an angry voice. 'What do you think you're doing?'

I sat up to see a railway character glaring at me. I glared back. 'I'm trying to catch up on a bit of bloody sleep. What does it look like?'

'Well, you can't sleep here—it's not allowed.'

'Who the hell says so?'

'I do, and if you don't roll that swag up I'll call the police.' He marched off, full of his own importance.

I thought things over. If the petty dictator was right, I didn't have enough money left to waste on a fine, so reluctantly I rolled up my swag and put it on the last seat on the platform. I sat down and, using it as a pillow, I was soon asleep. My tormentor must have checked up on me again, for he was not finished with me yet. I was rudely awakened by a rough hand on my shoulder.

I sat up abruptly to see him standing beside a large policeman. The copper looked me over and turned to my persecutor. 'Is this the trouble-maker?' he asked.

'Yes, that's him! That's him!'

The policeman turned his attention to me again. 'Right, what's your name? And what are you doing here?'

I told him my name and added bitterly that I was hoping to get a bit of sleep. He digested that and then advised me sternly that I should have booked into a hotel. He added that he could provide me with accommodation if necessary.

To hell with it, I thought, attack is always the best defence. I stood up. 'Are the pubs open here in the middle of the bloody night? I just got off the northern mail and I'm catching the train to Cloncurry tomorrow. Lock me up if you want to—as long as I can get away from that officious bastard, I might get some sleep.'

'There,' the railway man said, 'I told you.'

The copper turned to him and told him to shut up. He looked me over again. 'Watch your language. What are you going to do in Cloncurry?'

I said I was going to get a job ringing.

'You don't look like a ringer. Where did you work last?'

I had to admit he had a point. I was in town clothes and a long spell down South had given me the pallor of a city dweller. I told him where I had last worked, and pointed out that I wasn't in a stockcamp at the moment.

'What's the sergeant's name in Boulia?' he fired at me. I thanked God for a good memory and gave him the answer.

'Right, show me your rail ticket and some identification.'

I pulled the ticket out of my back pocket and handed it to him, together with my birth certificate. The railway man was getting fidgety, no doubt waiting impatiently for me to be hauled off to the clink. The policeman handed me back my ticket and certificate. He pushed his cap back and spoke.

'Well, you've got a big day ahead of you tomorrow. If I was you, I'd stretch out on that seat.' He paused. 'And I'd get a blanket out of your swag—it may turn a bit chilly towards morning.'

'But! But!' spluttered the railway man.

The policeman gave him a withering look. 'Don't you have anything better to do than harass a bonafide traveller?' he said coldly, and left us.

I grinned at the discomforted railway man and bade him goodnight.

I did better than pull out a blanket, I unrolled my swag on the seat and slept blissfully until I was awakened by the morning bustle on the platform. Pulling a clean set of clobber out of my swag, I made for the station showers. There for two and sixpence I freshened up, and leaving my swag at the cloakroom, I was ready for breakfast.

A lot has changed with rail travel over the past 50 years, not all for the good. The refreshment room at the Townsville station was the size of a hotel dining room. Crisp white table linen covered the tables, which were set with heavy silverware and china all bearing the QGR brand. A waitress in uniform ambled up, gave me the breakfast menu and took my order.

After a plate of rolled oats followed by steak and eggs, I sat back, rolled a smoke and poured myself another drink of tea from the silver-plated teapot. I was at peace with the world and outside the sun was shining. After paying for the meal, I decided to have a look around the town. The pubs weren't open as yet but the shops were trading and the streets were crowded. I wandered around until 10 o'clock then walked into the first pub I came to.

I ordered a half rum and cast an eye over the clientele. The bar was empty save for an unhappy-looking individual who was leaning on the bar and cradling a half empty rum glass. A battered hat was pulled down over his unshaven features and he had the slightly dishevelled look of a bushman on a spree. I finished my drink and invited him to join me. He looked at me suspiciously, then seeing that I too was drinking rum, he sidled down the bar. I introduced myself and told him I was on my way to Cloncurry. He nodded and said, 'Yeah, not a bad place, the Curry. I wish to Christ I was there now.'

I gave him a hard look, expecting him to put the fangs into me for money. 'What's the trouble?' I asked him.

He pushed his hat back. 'I arrived from the Charters Towers yesterday. I'm booked into one of the pubs here, but I don't remember which bloody one, so I'm on a pub crawl until I find it.'

I asked him where he had spent the night. He grinned ruefully and told me he had got on the piss and the coppers had locked him up for being drunk and disorderly. I laughed and related how I had very nearly joined him. After he had shouted, we strolled up to another pub in search of his room. At the fourth hotel we went into, my companion looked around and shook his head. 'No, this isn't the place,' he said despondently. 'I should have stayed in that bloody stockcamp.'

'Why did you leave?'

'Because of a bloody jackaroo head stockman. I ended up knocking the bastard arse over head and got the sack.'

Just then the publican came over to us. 'I didn't see you at dinner last night, Bill,' he said to my dejected mate.

Bill looked at him in astonishment. 'You mean, I'm booked in here?'

Mine host assured him that he was indeed a guest of the hotel. Bill let out a loud 'You bloody beaut', then, turning to me, said, 'Hang on here. I'll go and have a clean up and then I'll shout you a feed in the dining room.' He was almost to the stairs when he stopped and looked back. 'Hey! What room am I in?'

The publican told him and walked away shaking his head.

After about 20 minutes Bill came downstairs. He was freshly shaven, clad in clean clothes and generally looked like a new man. Lunch proved to be an enjoyable meal. My new-found companion was now in top form and regaled me with the shortcomings of the incompetent head stockman. The meal finished, we strolled outside, where I bade Bill farewell and advised him to sleep in his own bed that night. He grinned broadly.

'I'm going to give the grog away,' he declared. 'And see if I can get on to a sheila.'

Looking at the new Bill, I reckoned he had a chance at that. I sauntered back towards the railway station. As the train did not leave until after four o'clock, I took my time. Passing a stock and station agency, I noticed a sign in the window: 'Stockmen wanted', it proclaimed. I had never had the need to canvas agents for work, but curiosity got the better of me. I walked in and stood at the counter. A youngish chap came over and I told him I had seen the notice in the window. He looked me over. 'Have you done any stockwork?'

I assured him that I had.

'This is cattle work—do you have any references?'

'No, I've never needed references to get a job. Once you're known out further, that's good enough.'

I told him where I had worked and added I was on my way to Cloncurry.

'Well,' he said, 'they are looking for three stockmen on Lorraine, that's between Cloncurry and Burketown. I employed two chaps this morning—you can go out with them.'

He told me I would have to catch the train from the Curry to Dobbyn, then get a ride on the Burketown mail truck. He then got some details from me so he could wire the manager of my impending arrival, and dismissed me. I went away quite happy. I had a job in the Gulf and it meant I would not have to hang about the Curry looking for work.

Arriving at the railway station, I redeemed my swag and bought an Ellery Queen mystery book. I then settled down to a quiet read until the time came to board the western mail train. I noticed two young chaps dressed in ringers' garb on the platform and decided they must be the other two going to Lorraine. They were obviously mates and as they seemed happy in their own company I returned to my book.

I always enjoyed train travel, but being on the western mail was not a new experience, as I had made the trip a number of times when going further west. Despite this, I found myself absorbed in the passing countryside. Those days there were many gangs of fettlers along the length of the Queensland railway lines. Whenever a mail train passed a gang, the men would line up beside the track with cries of 'Paper, Paper'. It was the latest newspapers they were after. Most of the passengers obliged by tossing the papers out of the window. Sometimes if the train was making its way up a gradient you could hand the required reading matter to them personally.

The trip out to Cloncurry was fairly uneventful. Upon leaving the train, which was now heading for Mount Isa, I inquired about the Dobbyn rattler. God willing, I was informed, it would leave the following morning. I got the impression that the staff regarded the Dobbyn train as a bit of a joke. Back on the platform, I ran into the lads who were going to Lorraine with me. We yarned for a while, and I gathered they had never been this far north before. They appeared to be treating the whole thing as a bit of an adventure. I knew it would be an experience that would tax both their ability and their resilience but decided to let them find out for themselves. Picking up my swag, I walked to the nearest pub and booked a bed for the night.

The town of Cloncurry has always interested me. It has had a fascinating and turbulent history. Ernest Henry, who found copper in the area in 1867 and later established the Great Australian mine, has always been regarded as the founder of Cloncurry. The district was rich in minerals, and many mines were soon in operation in the area. These mines included the Gilded Rose, a gold show some 12 kilometres from the town, which was established after a short-lived alluvial rush at Soldier's Cap. Other mines in the district gave rise to towns like Selwyn, Kuridala, Duchess and Dobbyn. Some of these once-booming towns have struggled on and survived due to pastoral activity.

In January 1883 Sub Inspector Beresford was killed by the Kalkadoon tribe, which held sway in the district for some time. At one point there were fears that Cloncurry would be raided by the warlike Kalkadoons. In March 1884 Sub Inspector Frederick Urquhart was appointed to take control of the native police in the area. Widely experienced in dealing with Aborigines, Urquhart soon had the situation under control. The spearing of Powell, a part owner of Carlton Hills, proved to be the rock on which the Kalkadoons perished. Urquhart, together with graziers like Kennedy, went out and broke the power of the Kalkadoons.

Apart from its mining history, Cloncurry has always been the quintessential cattleman's town. The area contains a lot of rough country, and rough country always produces smart men. Over the years Cloncurry has also been the home of many characters as rough as the terrain—men like Galloping Jones, who regarded cattle duffing as a game rather than a crime. The Kajabbi and Dobbyn district has always had a reputation for lawlessness. Shortly before I started on Lorraine there was a double shooting in the area. The incident was put down to murder/suicide, but many of the locals questioned the verdict.

For many years Cloncurry hosted magnificent horse sales. I have seen hundreds of horses put through the yards, with buyers from many parts of Australia bidding for them. When a site was being sought for the Stockmen's Hall of Fame, Cloncurry threw its collective hat into the ring. I was living in the town then and was a member of a deputation formed to establish its claim. Cloncurry's bid proved to be unsuccessful, with the Hall of Fame going to Longreach, but that was of course years after my going to Lorraine.

In my room at the Leichhardt Hotel I unrolled my swag, emptied the pocket and went through my clothes. It was obvious I needed some new work clobber, and now that I had a job to go to, I could afford the outlay. Going downstairs, I strolled around the town until I found myself at Power's Emporium. When I left that well-known establishment, I had all the gear I needed, together with the information that there was a cattle duffing case in progress at the courthouse. As I was at a loose end, I presented myself at the hall of justice and spent an enthralling few hours there. The defendant, one Billy Mitchell, was on trial for duffing cattle from Coolullah Station. Mitchell had no country of his own, but ran a thriving herd on the Dobbyn common. Les Teece, the head stockman at Coolullah, was giving evidence when I sat down. It was soon evident to me that Mitchell would not be escaping justice as Harry Redford had.

I left Mitchell to his fate in the Cloncurry court house and returned to the Leichhardt Hotel. Next morning, dressed in brand new riding gear, I caught the train to Dobbyn. Dressed as I was, I knew I'd be letting myself in for some baiting at Lorraine. Blokes who turned up to a job in new gear were usually regarded as being as inexperienced as their clothes. Although initiation in the workplace is fairly uncommon in Australia, we've all heard of the new apprentice being sent to get a tin of striped paint. Jokes like that were often played on new chums on stations, but the only serious test of ability was the 'trial horse'—a horse that could buck a little and was used to establish the experience of a new man. The practice was neither company nor managerial policy and depended largely on the personality of the head stockman.

When the three of us arrived at the station, we were greeted in friendly manner by the assembled ringers, but I noticed a few nudges and winks directed towards me. Everyone was going down to the Leichhardt River for a swim. The other two new blokes jumped at the idea, but I decided to do some washing in preparation for work, which was to start the next day. The Lorraine lads seemed disappointed—no doubt they had something in mind for my benefit.

After hanging my clothes out, I strolled down to where the stockcamp lads were having a great time in the river, diving out of a boat made out of the belly tank of an aircraft. I declined the offer to join them and sat down on the bank to await events. I knew sooner or later I was going to end up in the river, but was determined it would be on my terms. One of the other new arrivals asked me to look after a camera he had, so I carefully put my hat over it, surreptitiously slipping my tobacco under the hat as well. Then, taking my boots off, I made a great point of paring my toenails with my pocket knife.

After a few minutes, they showed their hand. The boat edged in to the bank. 'If you can't swim, come for a ride in the boat. We'll look after you.'

I almost laughed. 'Righto,' I said, and stepped into the boat.

I knew they would tip the boat over out in the middle of the hole, and I was not disappointed. They started skylarking, jumping in and out, and finally over she went. I dived off the high side as it tipped and, swimming underwater, headed for the bank. I broke the surface behind a canopy of drooping tea-tree boughs, then sat on the bank and watched as their mirth turned to concern. Very soon concern became blind panic as they dived in an attempt to find my body.

Deciding that the joke had gone far enough, I stood up and went and sat down by my hat. When they finally saw me, one of them whom I had picked out as a smart ringer, swam over to the bank. He stood up and looked at me. 'You bastard! You put it over us.' There was mingled relief and astonishment in his voice.

I grinned at him. 'Yes, I'm not quite as wet behind the ears as you blokes thought.'

He climbed up the bank and sat down beside me. I rolled a smoke and handed it to him, then rolled one for myself and lit them both. He took a drag on the cigarette and declared, 'I reckon you've been around a bit, eh?'

I nodded and told him where I had been. We yarned for a while about the various stations we had worked on, then returned together to the ringers' quarters. He became a good mate of mine; in fact, I got on well with all the ringers. They were a lively lot and it was one of the happiest camps I had ever worked in.

Next morning we were to muster workhorses for the coming cattle work. By keeping my ear to the ground, I had verified that Lorraine did have a trial horse. He was a bay gelding with a blaze face called Crocodile and, sure enough, when we got to the horse yards Crocodile was among our mounts. I half expected to be given him, but apparently I had already established my credentials. Crocodile was given to the tallest of the other new arrivals.

We saddled up and rode off, with the trial horse giving no clue to his real nature. When we had the workhorses mustered later that morning, however, Crocodile was among them and his saddle was empty. I was told that Crocodile was not a bad buckjumper, although quite capable of throwing a novice. Two of the ringers caught and unsaddled Crocodile, then, leading a quiet horse, rode back to find the missing lad. On their way, they came upon a gum tree with a message scratched on its white bark: 'Going down river to try and find station.'

They found the missing lad unharmed, and a red-faced young ringer joined us for the midday meal. That gum tree became known thereafter as Crocodile's tree.

That afternoon the horses were drafted and a string of five was given to each ringer. When two good-looking brown mares came into the pound yard, one, Rosette, was put into my string and the other, a nice-looking mare called Sea Breeze, was given to Keith Campbell. Keith was a member of a well-known Gulf family, and he and his brothers were all top horsemen.

Once we knew what horses had been allocated to us, we tidied up their tails and started shoeing them. I had just caught Rosette when Keith came over to me. 'What about swapping that brown mare for the one I've got?'

I was a bit surprised, for neither of us knew the horses and I thought Sea Breeze was the better-looking mare. He was keen to trade, though, and I finally agreed to the change.

After we finished shoeing next morning, we all gave our horses a ride in the yard. Most station horses those days would buck or at least pig jump when fresh. We were taking turns to ride them and when Keith saddled up Rosette I watched with interest. The mare pulled away before he could mount her and put on as good a display of buckjumping as I

The author as a young stockman in Queensland, the saddle was made by Billy Hock of Springsure.

had seen for a long time. I grinned at Keith, but he just shrugged his shoulders, caught the reins and swung into the saddle. He rode her easily in the yard, but once outside on the flat, she started bucking with a vengeance. Keith had no trouble riding her, but I was not sorry I had agreed to the exchange. Soft and out of condition as I was from a spell in the city, I doubt if I could have ridden her outside. I later saddled and rode Sea Breeze. She had a couple of goes at me, but she was not in Rosette's class.

The camp was going out to Cassady's camp next day and the horse plant was let go overnight in the station horse paddock. A grey gelding was put in the yard to use for running them in the next morning, and I was told by the head stockman it would be my job to do so. He also told me not to use a whip when riding the grey. I looked at him in disbelief, the horse paddock was fairly heavily timbered in places and a whip would make the job a lot easier.

'He's never been broken in to a whip?' I asked.

'No, you can't use a whip on him.'

'Well, the bastard will have one used on him tomorrow morning.'

At daylight I caught and saddled the grey, then, throwing my whip over his wither, I mounted and rode to the back of the paddock. I started horses back to the yards as I went and then cantered along the back fence. I swung the whip up and cracked it—and the grey exploded under me. As he hit the ground, I cracked it again. The next moment he went crashing into a tree, splitting my head open. Half blinded by the blood that was streaming down my face, I struggled to stay in the saddle. The grey was now galloping along behind the horse mob. I just made it to the yards, where two of the ringers helped me out of the saddle and over to a patch of lawn. I must have lost a fair amount of blood, as they had to hose down both the horse and my saddle. I was helped over to the quarters, where I wrapped a towel around my head and got out of my clothes, which were growing stiff with dried blood.

I was lying back on my bunk when the head stockman came in. He looked at me. 'Well, are you satisfied?'

I gave a weak grin. 'Oh, you can use a whip on the bastard all right, but you want to bail out f... smartly afterwards.'

I stayed on my bunk all day. The flying doctor, when contacted, advised plenty of fluids. As the stockcamp had departed, I was plied with sweet tea by one of the manager's daughters. My head was never stitched but healed up quite quickly, although I pulled pieces of wood out of my scalp for a number of years afterwards.

A couple of days later I rejoined the camp to a chorus of 'Did you bring your whip with you?'

I enjoyed my time in the Lorraine stockcamp. On ocasions when we were in at the head station, a few of us gave an impromptu night time concert on the flying doctor's network. One chap played the gum leaf, another the comb; I played a mouth organ, and Jack Durham coached music out of a rare instrument he made out of an oil can and some tie wire. They were a great bunch of blokes.

Towards the end of the year the mustering finished and the stockcamp moved to the head station. Many of the ringers made plans for the holidays later. Taffy, who had been cooking in the stockcamp, took over the men's kitchen and cooked for us there. Most of us got on well with him. A swarthy-looking individual, Taffy claimed to be a Welshman, and would offer to fight anyone who doubted his word. A week after we got to the station Taffy pulled out and caught the Burketown mail that would connect with the train to Cloncurry.

An hour or so after the mail truck had gone, the manager, George Schultz, came over to me. He asked me if I wanted to go for a drive, explaining that he had to put a parcel on the train. I wondered briefly why he had not put it on the mail truck, but said I'd be happy to go with him as a gate opener.

We arrived at Dobbyn with the Cloncurry train standing at the station. When we walked onto the platform, Taffy was standing there with a rather pregnant-looking swag. As soon as he saw us, he ran over to George, crying, 'I'm sorry, Boss. I didn't mean to take that gear. I don't know what came over me.'

George looked at him and said, 'Right, Taffy, show me what you've got?'

The terrified Taffy went to his swag. He unrolled it and half of the cooking gear from the ringers' kitchen fell out onto the platform. I left Taffy appealing to the manager not to hand him over to the police and carried the assorted kitchen ware to the station vehicle. George did not charge Taffy, but he did tell him he'd never get another job in the Gulf. We watched a deflated Taffy depart with an equally deflated swag.

George Schultz was a man who kept his own council. I don't know to this day if we went to Dobbyn because he suspected Taffy. Now and again on the way back to Lorraine George hummed a little tune. It was vaguely familiar, but I could not place it. Then it hit me. He was humming the old nursery rhyme: 'Taffy was a Welshman, Taffy was a thief'.

All Among the Wool

After spending two stock seasons in the Gulf, I left Augustus Downs in October. My younger brother and I had arranged to go down South for a holiday. Alan was breaking in horses on a station around Clermont and we planned to meet in Mackay, then, after a few days at home, we would head to Sydney to let off a bit of steam. However, the old adage 'The best laid plans of mice and men . . .' reared its hoary head the day before I left Augustus. I received a telegram from Alan saying he would not be ready for another month. Consequently, I found myself in a difficult situation; I could not afford to sit around spending money while I waited for Alan, and stockwork had all but finished.

I spent a couple of unrewarding days in Cloncurry, then caught a mixed train to Hughenden. This train, affectionately known to the locals as the 'Old Nineteen Down', duly delivered me at my destination. Heaving my swag on my shoulder, I walked up town and booked into a hotel. Hotels were the only accommodation for travellers those days; they made their money over the bar but were compelled by the licensing laws to provide rooms for the weary commercial travellers and others. They did so with no great enthusiasm

I dragged my swag up the stairs to the room I had been allocated and sat down on one of the beds. The room held two single beds, a large wooden wardrobe with one door askew and a washstand. Washstands were standard bedroom furniture those days. This one had a grimy mirror and a marble top holding a large china wash dish and a tall water pitcher. There was also a drinking glass on the marble top, in case a weary traveller should take the unlikely step of drinking water. Under the washstand was a badly cracked and chipped chamber pot. In the condition it was in, I doubted it would be of any use to any guest with a full bladder.

I found the showers at the end of a hall near the back stairs. The toilets were located in the backyard. The male facility consisted of a galvanised iron shed housing two thunder boxes; the urinal was a concrete drain, and an iron fence provided privacy, but it did not boast a roof. I considered the hazards of reaching the toilets from the bedrooms in the middle of the night, and came to the conclusion that the chamber pot may not yet be redundant.

I had a clean up and wandered down to the bar. It was Friday afternoon and the place was crowded. I ordered a beer, and when I got the chance, I asked the barman about the work situation. He told me there was little stockwork about, but that the shearing sheds were still busy. The opinion I held of sheep and shearing was typical of all cattlemen—sheep were stupid and the only thing dumber than a sheep was a sheepman.

I had a few more beers, then when the dinner bell rang I wandered into the dining room. Though the accommodation in the bush pubs of that era might have been less than desirable, the tucker was first rate. I saddled up to a huge meal of roast mutton plus roast potatoes and pumpkin, garnished by a rich brown gravy. I have never been keen on desserts, but the aroma of the steam pudding and custard almost seduced me.

After dinner I returned to my room to find a battered suitcase under the other bed. Shortly after, my room-mate appeared. He was a rather rotund individual of middle age with a round, cheerful face and greying hair. He said he was a woolroller and that I could call him Blackie. I introduced myself and told him I was looking for stockwork. Blackie made a sympathetic noise then excused himself with: 'I've got to study the form now'. He opened the paper he had been carrying at the racing guide pages and got to work with a pencil.

I lay back on the bed and thought things over. It looked as though I would have to go in further to pick up work. My reverie was broken by my room-mate, who stood up saying, 'I'm going downstairs to get some money on before the price shortens. I'll see you when I get back.'

Blackie duly returned. He sat on his bed and looked at me. 'So you're looking for a job. Why don't you try the shearing sheds?'

I looked at him in surprise. 'I've never seen a sheep at close quarters and I know nothing at all about shearing.'

Blackie looked me over. 'You're young and fit. You'd get a job picking up.'

'Picking up what?' I asked him.

He laughed. 'Picking up fleeces, of course. When a shearer finishes shearing a sheep, he leaves the wool on the shearing board. It's the picker-up's job to gather it and throw it out on the wool table.'

'How the hell do you pick up a heap of wool?'

Blackie looked disgusted. 'Here, I'll show you.' He opened his port and dragged out a none-too-clean towel. 'Now, the fleece is upside down when it comes off,' he said, and threw the towel across the floor in front of him. 'Now, watch what I do.' He straightened the towel a little, put his left foot up to the near side and then, reaching forward, he picked up the far side between the thumb and two fingers of each hand. He then brought both hands back together and picked up the folded towel at his foot.

'That's all there is to picking it up, but now you have to throw it out right side up like this. He walked over and threw it on the bed. He was still holding the edges between thumbs and fingers and this had the effect of flipping the towel over so that it landed with the other side up. He looked at me.

'There you are, there's nothing to it. Here, have a go.'

The towel landed on the floor and I attempted to emulate Blackie's smooth handling of the make-believe fleece. After 20 minutes of practice and advice, I was picking the towel up and throwing it out with confidence. Blackie, obviously pleased with his pupil, told me I'd have no trouble getting a job in the sheds.

'I'll tell you what,' he said after a bit of thought. 'The contractor I work for is looking for a shedhand. I'll give you a break to him tomorrow. I reckon you'll be as right as rain once you get the hang of it.'

True to his word, Blackie introduced me to the shearing contractor on Saturday afternoon. When he heard I was looking for a job, but was inexperienced, he looked me over and said, 'Well, I'll give you a start—if you're willing to learn, you'll be right. We'll pick you up with Blackie tomorrow afternoon.'

Later I asked Blackie if I needed any special gear. 'No,' that worthy replied. 'Just make sure you take sandshoes or gym boots.'

I looked at him in dismay. I owned neither, and the shops were closed.

I learnt from Blackie that I would be picking up for five shearers. The gun, a chap named Matthews, was shearing more than 200 a day, and the others were not too far behind him. I was going to be handicapped by wearing riding boots, but was prepared to give it a go. I was to learn to my dismay, however, that picking up newly shorn fleeces was not as easy as handling Blackie's towel.

Next afternoon I threw my swag onto the contractor's truck, and my life as a rouseabout began. There were a couple of other shedhands on the vehicle, including Blackie. The shearers, apparently, could afford their own transport. At the shearers' quarters I found there was a spare bed in Blackie's room, so I claimed it, keen not to lose contact with my adviser. The evening meal was an eye opener for me. There was a choice of three main courses and two desserts. Afterwards I asked Blackie if Sunday dinner was regarded as a special occasion. My room-mate threw back his head and laughed. 'No, Simmo, that was a bit below the standard of meals during the working week. Shearers are hungry bastards. But they do work hard.'

As we lay on our beds that night Blackie gave me a rundown of the shearing game. It started, he told me, when a grazier and a shearing contractor signed a contract in which the contractor agreed to shear the flock for a set price per head. The contractor then employed shearers who shore for so much per hundred sheep and a wool presser, who agreed to press the clip for so much a bale. The rest of the team were waged or salaried workers. Two of the team were specialists. The wool classer was a semi-professional who graded the wool into various qualities; the expert, another skilled man, kept the shearers' cutters sharp. The other waged men were called rouseabouts and included penners-up, pickers-up, piece-pickers and woolrollers. Then there was the cook. The shearers had a big say in the hiring of the cook and he could be sent packing if they voted him out. The contractor kept an eye on the whole operation. I asked Blackie about the machinery and he explained that an engine-driven shaft ran the length of the shearing board; friction wheels above each shearer's stand drove a flexible enclosed shaft connected to the handpieces used to do the shearing. These friction wheels could be engaged or released by pulling a rope beside each stand. Armed with this knowledge, I went to sleep.

I thought Blackie may have been pulling my leg about the tucker, but after a multi-choice breakfast next morning I was convinced. As we left to go to the shearing shed, Blackie turned to me. 'Have you got your ticket?'

'Ticket! What ticket?'

'Your union ticket, the AWU ticket. You do have one?'

'Yes, it's in my gear somewhere. I'll see if I can find it.'

After rooting around in my swag, I finally found the ticket I had taken out on Augustus. It was just as well I did, for at the shed there was a call for a show of tickets. There was no place for scabs in the sheds those days.

On the job I was more or less under the orders of the wool classer. He was an Irish Australian, and a bit of an old woman. He watched my attempts to pick up the first fleece, then pushed me aside and showed me how I should be doing it. To be honest, I found it extremely difficult to handle the fleece and even harder to throw the damned thing out in the prescribed way on the wool table. It was also part of my job to take a tar pot to any shearer who nicked a sheep and to sweep the loose wool up from the shearing board. For quite a while there was more wool on the board than thrown onto the wool table.

By the end of the first run I was beginning to get the hang of it, although I was often late in getting fleeces out of the way before the shearers started on another sheep. Four of them would kick the fleece to one side so I could get at it, but the man on the far stand shore on top of it, making it a bloody mess. He was a cranky old bastard who had been a gun in his day but was now the slowest of the lot. I cursed him under my breath, swearing I would bide my time and get even.

At the end of the day I was buggered. Ringers are in pretty good nick, but in picking up, a completely different set of muscles are called on. That night I was asleep almost before my head touched the pillow. Next morning I threw my riding boots off and worked in my socks. I found it a lot easier, although I did pick up a few splinters from the shearing board. I threw the last fleece out before smoko and it landed perfectly. Blackie grinned and gave me a thumbs up. I had never had time before to see what happened then, so I watched with interest as Blackie and another chap picked the dags and broken pieces from the fleece then rolled it up for the classer to inspect. The classer gave it the once over and threw it in one of a number of bins denoting quality.

By the end of the third day I felt I was getting on top of the job. Despite a few blisters and splinters, I was beginning to enjoy the bustle and rivalry on the shearing board. That night after a hot shower and a first class meal, Blackie continued with my education. Shearers and rouseabouts had little in common, he said, and this arose because of the different way they were paid. Being on contract, shearers were only paid while they were shearing. If they had to stop because of an engine failure or wet weather the money stopped. Rouseabouts, on the other hand, were on wages and were paid during any hold-up in shearing. Blackie told me that an old Afghan he once knew summed it up in a little ditty he used to sing. It went like this:

Shearer man like plenty butter
Moffat comb and Cooper cutter,
Rouseabout like plenty joke
Rain come up and engine broke.

I asked Blackie about hold-ups due to rain and what the real problem was. He sat up on his bed and rolled a smoke.

'Well,' he replied, 'wet sheep are supposed to give shearers arthritis. If there is any doubt, the shearers vote on it. If they vote wet sheep, then shearing stops. Mind you, a lot depends on how cashed up they are. I've seen 'em vote wet sheep after a heavy dew; I've also seen 'em vote dry when the bloody frogs are jumping out of the fleeces.'

Blackie told me that shearers did not approve of women in the sheds. If a female was seen approaching, the cry of 'Ducks on the pond' went up. He added that shearers were a superstitious bunch, but did not elaborate. Later I was to find out just how true this was.

Matthews was still well ahead on numbers shorn. As a shearer finished a sheep, he pushed it down a shute leading to a pen that held only his shorn sheep. At the end of the day a tally was made, so everyone knew the score. I was now faster at picking up, although the old coot at the far stand still caught me occasionally. He would just look at me and say, 'Well, you'll just have to smarten up a bit.'

At the weekend I went into Hughenden and bought myself a pair of gym boots. Now, I thought to myself, that old bastard is about to get his. I held off until Wednesday, when big strong wethers were being shorn and the old shearer had his hands full. My moment came when he came out of the pen backwards, dragging a big wether. I picked up his last fleece and, crouching down, moved sidewards, leaving my right leg outstretched. He fell over it backwards and the big wether kicked hell out of him before it escaped. He stood up and glared at me. I glared back and said, 'Well, you'll just have to smarten up a bit,' and left him.

I had now become quite an expert at the job and was growing in confidence. The shearers weren't a bad bunch, but one night an incident occurred that made me question their sanity. I was lying on my bunk after tea and Blackie was occupied elsewhere. I pulled my mouth organ out of the pocket of my swag and started to play it. A few minutes later a commotion started in the quarters; men were shouting and walls were being thumped. I imagined the shearers were engaging in a bit of horseplay, until two irate-looking shearers appeared in my doorway.

'Stop playing that bloody mouth organ,' one of them demanded.

I looked at them in astonishment. 'What the hell are you talking about?'

'Stop playing that blasted thing or we'll jam it down your throat.'

I stood up. 'Will you now,' I said.

Just then Blackie arrived on the scene. 'I'll handle this,' he told them.

After they'd gone Blackie looked at me. 'You never told me you played the mouth organ?'

'So bloody what?'

'Hang on, cool down a bit. You remember me telling you that shearers were a superstitious lot?'

Mystified, I nodded.

'Well, they think that playing the mouth organ will bring rain.'

I looked at Blackie in disbelief. 'You're joking?'

'No, the silly bastards really believe it. You've seen their reaction.'

To me it seemed incredible that grown men could believe such nonsense; it was not only childish but stupid. Next morning the contractor buttonholed me. 'Look, I'm happy with your work, but I'll have to ask you not to play that mouth organ again. I like a happy team and that does upset them.'

I reluctantly agreed, but could not resist having a dig.

'Do you have to put money under their bloody pillows when they lose a tooth?' I asked.

He gave me a hard look then walked off. Later I told Blackie of the encounter. He called me a cheeky bastard and said I was lucky to still have a job.

After two and a half weeks the shed cut out and we were all paid off. Back in Hughenden, Blackie, who seemed to know everything, said he had heard we were going out to another shed. As always he was right, and the following Sunday afternoon the shearing team assembled at the new station. There was a larger flock to shear and the contractor had put on another shearer.

'Christ!' I said to Blackie. 'I'll have to pull my finger out here.' He just laughed and advised me that if six shearers were engaged there had to be two men picking up.

This turned out to be the case. I got on well with the new picker-up, a lad from Charters Towers. With two of us working, it was a breeze. We took turns in working the three far stands and kept racing each other to send the fleeces flying out onto the wool table. However, on one occasion Blackie failed to get out of the way of a fleece thrown by the new lad, and the wool classer threw up his hands in horror. Blackie backed out from under the fleece and said dryly, 'If you young fellows like running so much, I might have a word to the cook about putting some jalap in your tucker.'

We did steady up a bit. I did not want to fall out with my mentor. We finished the first week with Matthews still well ahead on the tally board. The new shearer, a young chap from New South Wales, put it to him for a while, but then Matthews forged ahead.

I was almost sorry when I heard that the shed would finish up on the Monday two weeks after we had started. On the Friday a young chap who was horse breaking on the place asked me if I was going in to town on the last weekend. I told him I wasn't, as we were due to finish on the Monday. He then asked if I would mind riding out a colt to muster the last of the sheep. He explained he had two freshly broken horses that were now ready for a bit of work. I jumped at the chance to get on a horse again and agreed to meet him at the horse yards after lunch on Sunday.

At two o'clock I strolled down to the yards, where the breaker was mouthing two colts. He seemed relieved to see me, and leaving what he was doing, walked over with me to another yard.

'There they are,' he said. 'You can take your pick. Both are going okay.'

I got a bridle, and walking up to a bay filly, caught her without any trouble. She humped a bit when I girthed her up so I led her around until she relaxed. When breaking in, it is best not to let horses buck. They learn bad habits quickly enough without being encouraged. When the breaker was ready, we both mounted and, after giving our mounts a ride in the yard, joined the musterers. The filly I was riding had a good mouth and seemed quite tractable. It was not a big paddock we were mustering and we soon began putting the sheep together. I noticed a small mob going for their lives in the wrong direction and, seeing it as a chance to give the filly a good gallop, set off after them. I had nearly caught up with them when something flashed by my mount's ears, and a telephone line hit me in the face. It almost dragged me out of the saddle, but I managed to regain my seat and keep the filly under control. My face, however, was a bloody mess. The wire had lifted the skin on the left side of my face from jawline to forehead and I could not see out of my left eye.

I rode back to the mob and later let the filly go at the yards. The young horse breaker was both concerned and apologetic, but I assured him it was not his fault. It was the second time in two years I had been involved in a similar accident, but the first, at Lorraine, had been entirely my own fault because of over confidence. Here, however, I felt the station was guilty of carelessness bordering on criminal negligence. I was leaving the yards when the manager, who had seen something was wrong, stopped me.

'Did that horse throw you?'

I glared at him with my one good eye. 'No, the filly didn't throw me, that bloody phone line of yours nearly took my f... head off.' I then proceeded to give him my opinion of sheep stations in general and his in particular.

'But, but,' he spluttered, 'you went out of your own volition.'

'That's true, but you'll be hearing from my solicitors,' I said and walked off.

It was an idle threat, but it sounded good. I knew as I was not on the station books I could not even get workers' compensation.

When I walked in to my room, Blackie, who was half asleep on his bed, sat up. 'Jesus Christ! What have you done to yourself?'

I explained what had happened and he rabbited around in his suitcase and came up with a battered-looking first aid kit. My left eye was completely closed, but facial injuries always look worse than they are. Blackie patched me up with bandages and sticking plaster and I went to the evening meal looking like the phantom of the opera.

The shed cut out at three o'clock the next day, with Matthews still the gun. We packed up and drove into Hughenden. It was to be my first and last encounter with sheep. There was a letter from Alan for me at the hotel. He had arrived at Mackay and was rearing to go. Three days later I joined him.

Sources

Death on the Barkly

North Queensland Register, 24/10/1883.

Adelaide Advertiser, 15/11/1883, 16/11/1883, 17/11/1883, 29/11/1883.

Northern Territory Times and Gazette, 5/1/1884.

Booth, Edwin C, *Australia in the 1870s*, facsimile edition, Uhr Smith, Sydney, c1975.

Buchanan, Bobbie, *In the Tracks of Old Bluey*, Central Queensland University Press, Rockhampton, Qld, 1996.

Buchanan, Gordon, *Packhorse and Waterhole*, Angus and Robertson, Sydney, 1933.

Cole, Tom, *Hell West and Crooked*, William Collins Pty Ltd, Sydney, 1988.

Downer, Sydney, *Patrol Indefinite*, Rigby Ltd, Adelaide, 1963.

Hill, Ernestine, *The Territory*, Angus and Robertson, Sydney, 1951.

Morey, Ted, article in *Northern Territory Newsletter*, May 1977.

Teece, Cecil and Pike, Glenville, *Voice from the Wilderness*, published by authors, 1978.

Interviews with Cecil Teece of Normanton, Qld and Peter Treloar of Delaney's Creek, Qld.

Phone interview with Ron Easey of Petrie, Qld.

Where the Pelican Builds

Australian Dictionary of Biography, Vol. 3, Melbourne University Press, 1969.

Blachall, correspondent of the *Queenslander*, 5/10/1878.

Carr-Boyd, reports in the *Queenslander*, 7/9/1878, 5/4/1879, 12/4/1879, 26/4/1879, 3/5/1879, 17/5/1879.

Clune, Frank, 'Skeletons in the Sand'. *Short Story Magazine*, December 1948.

Mackanes, George and Mackanes Joan S. 'The Wide Brown Land' Angus and Roberston Sydney 1954—An anthology.

Oldtimer, report in the *Queenslander*, 5/10/1878.

Powell, Alan, *Far Country*, Melbourne University Press, 1982.

Dangerous Waters

North Queensland Register, 8/1/1917.

North Queensland Register, 10/3/1945.

Cairns Post, 27/11/1951, 28/11/1951.

Bagnell, Fred, *North Queensland Cavalcade*, published by author, Charters Towers, 1979.

Kerry Kendall, unpublished account of incidents at Topsy Creek and Keelbottom Creek.

Interviews with the following people: Laurie Hansen of Finch Hatton, Qld; Noel Thompson of D'Aguilar, Qld; Keith Haughton of Narangba, Qld; Bob Isles of Redcliffe, Qld; Colin Campbell of Mitchell, Qld; Bob Howard of Caboolture, Qld; Lucky Forrester of Strathpine, Qld; Eugene Costin of Brunette Downs, NT.

Phone interviews with Jim 'Ringer' Edwards of Gin Gin, WA and Bill Alexander of Marion Downs, Qld.

After Buchanan

Cusack, Thomas, unpublished account of his droving trips in 1961–62.

Laffin, Laurence James and Dargush, Marion Joan, *The J.A. Laffin Story*, published by authors, Ipswich, Qld, 1996.

Pike, Glenville, *Frontier Territory*, published by author, 1972.

Interviews with the following ex-drovers: Bob Isles of Redcliffe, Qld; Noel 'Pic' Willetts of Camooweal, Qld; Herb Heumiller of Barcaldine, Qld; Ian Tait of Koumala, Qld; the late Jack Gardner of Caloundra, Qld; the late Bobby McDonald of Barcaldine, Qld; Rodney Mosted of Camooweal, Qld; Noel Thompson of D'Aguilar, Qld; and Peter Isles of Redcliffe, Qld.

Prizes for Riders

Interview with Sam Fuller Jnr.

Roughriders of the Bush

Buchanan, Bobbie, *In the Tracks of Old Bluey*, Central Queensland University Press, Rockhampton, Qld, 1996.

Cole, Tom, *Hell West and Crooked*, William Collins Pty Ltd, Sydney, 1988.

Cronau, E.R., article in *People* magazine, February 1961.

Delhunty, Larry, article in *North Queensland Register*, 22/2/1990.

Green, Jean and Fitzgerald, James, *McLennan's Way*, Hesperian Press, Carlisle, WA, 1994.

McConville, Ray, *McConville's Wild Australians*, published by author, Myrtleford, Vic, 1997.

Mitchell, Gregory, article in *Hoofs and Horns*, December 1995.

Morey, Ted, article in the *Northern Territory Newsletter*, July 1997.

Orme, Les, article in *Man Magazine*, August 1949.

Pike, Glenville, *Round the Campfire*, Pinevale Publications, Mareeba.

Tatz, Colin, article in *Hoofs and Horns*, July 1996.

The late Frank Uhr, letter to the *North Queensland Register*, some 50 years ago.

Information contributed by the following people:

Jack Cunningham of Brisbane, Qld; Mrs Lola Rowe of Mildura, Vic; Rod Bellette of Patterson Lakes, Vic; Jim 'Ringer' Edwards of Gin Gin, WA; Merv Rogers of Charters Towers, Qld; Luke McCall of Batlow, NSW; Bob Isles of Redcliffe, Qld; Barry Desailly of North Ward, Qld; Les Huddy of Mt Isa, Qld; Gordon Gaffney of Tamworth, NSW; Ray Webster of Landsborough, Qld; George Booth Jnr of Port Douglas, Qld; Mick Bailey of Broken Hill, NSW; Tidly Treffett of Charters Towers, Qld; Alex Logan of Kumbia, Qld; Ernie McCarthy of Pine Creek, NT; Eddie Hackman of Rockhampton, Qld; Herb Heumiller of Barcaldine, Qld; Ian Tait of Koumala, Qld; the late Jack Gardner of Caloundra, Qld; Bob Kirk of Herbert Downs, Qld; Mal Debney of Glenormiston Station, Qld; the late Walter Lloyd of Boulia, Qld; Bob Howard of Caboolture, Qld; Ross Ratcliffe of The Willows, Qld; Jeff Simpson of Stanthorpe, Qld; Merv Thomas of Landsborough, Qld; Mick Thomas of Barcaldine, Qld; Noel Thompson of D'Aguilar, Qld; Barney Bellford of Eukey, Qld; the late Bobby McDonald of Barcaldine, Qld; the late Gilbert Macintosh of Mt Isa, Qld; Noel 'Pic' Willetts of Camooweal, Qld; John Chaplain of Cloncurry, Qld; Jack Drake of Eukey, Qld; Ab Teece of Cloncurry, Qld; Mrs Ada Devereaux of Brisbane, Qld; Colin Campbell of Mitchell, Qld; Ray Gillham of Suttor Creek Station, Qld; Lyn Craig of Eton, Qld; Graham

Murchie of Stanthorpe, Qld; Lloyd Linson-Smith of Oakey, Qld; Peter Isles of Redcliffe, Qld; Alex Long of Caboolture, Qld.

Characters and Hard Cases

Buchanan, Gordon, *Packhorse and Waterhole*, Angus and Robertson, Sydney, 1933.

Evert, Peter, unpublished article on Gidgee Taylor.

Lamond, G.A., *Tales of the Overland*, Hesperian Press, Victoria Park, WA, 1986.

Linklaker, William and Tapp, Linda, *Gather No Moss*, Macmillan of Australia, 1968.

Wild Men and Windlasses

A number of interviews with the late Fred Holm of Winton, Qld; interviews with the following people: the late Mrs Martyr Snr of Mayneside Station, Winton, Qld; Ron Bates of Gatton, Qld; Bill Moore of Redcliffe, Qld; and Graham McKerrow of Weona Station, Winton, Qld; Ion Idriess, Lightning Ridge.

Phone interview with Brian Holm of Winton, Qld and Matt Masterson of Mareeba, Qld.

Taped interview with Mick Cheadle of Millungra Station, Qld.

The Red Flash

Capricornian Opal Company's files.

A number of long interviews with Jeff Simpson, of Stanthorpe, Qld and Mick Cheadle, Millungra Station, Qld. Interviews with Graham McKerrow of Weona Station, Winton, Qld and the late Vince Evert of Winton, Qld.

North to the Gulf

Armstrong, R.E.M., *The Kalkadoons*, William Brooks & Co. Pty Ltd, Brisbane.

Fysh, Hudson, *Taming the North*, Angus and Robertson, Sydney, 2nd edition, 1950.